God's Irregular:
Arthur Shearly Cripps

A Rhodesian Epic

for D. T. A. Kantonea in friendship over the years.

13.V.80   Douglas V. Steere

God's Irregular:
Arthur Shearly Cripps

A Rhodesian Epic

DOUGLAS V. STEERE

LONDON
S·P·C·K

First published 1973
Reprinted 1973
S.P.C.K.
Holy Trinity Church
Marylebone Road
London NW1 4DU

Printed in Great Britain by
Fletcher & Son Ltd, Norwich

Distributed in the United States of America
by Pendle Hill Publications,
Wallingford, Pa 19086

SBN 281 02675 0

To our Rhodesian friends

Contents

Introduction

I once asked a Rhodesian African journalist and legislator to tell me frankly what the Africans who knew him thought of Arthur Shearly Cripps. He paused for a moment and then with a toss of his head, he replied, 'I think they loved him more than they love themselves.' In travelling about Rhodesia, my wife and I saw and talked with many of Cripps's African friends and my wife has always said that if in some way we had been able to photograph their faces as they lighted up when they talked of the one they called 'Baba Cripps', we could have shared a record of his place in their lives that would be far more convincing than any written account we might produce. In some mysterious way, Arthur Cripps had communicated with his African brethren that they were deeply and tangibly present to him and present to the One in whose service he came. And they took him to themselves. When I visited Cripps's grave in the nave of his little African-style church, there were fresh flowers in a little glass jug put there by some grateful African who had not forgotten. I was told by an African friend that the jug was seldom empty. His death was almost twenty years ago.

During the decade between the mid-fifties and the mid-sixties, we made a number of visits to Rhodesia, and in talking with people about recent Rhodesian history, we were always picking up bits of the Cripps legend. Both the white and the black communities were intrigued with the tales of his unusual conduct. It was not a commonplace, even in a pioneer country of an unusual and un-conventional type such as Rhodesia, to have this highly gifted Anglican priest-poet-missionary who was willing actually to iden-tify his life with that of the Mashona people, to be the Africans' fearless advocate both in Rhodesia and in Britain, and to be utterly expendable in their service.

The story as I pieced it together seemed to me to be unique and so gripping that I looked forward wistfully to a time of leave when we could search for the materials both in Rhodesia and in Britain that would light up this remarkable life, and then to set it down in the form of a biography.

As I went about the work, I discovered that the period of Arthur Cripps's service to Rhodesia which stretched from 1901 to 1952 actually covered all but a decade of the whole span of Rhodesian history up to the coming of the ill-fated Federation in 1953. This epic life of his, so full of strain and failure and troubles, as well as of joy and effective spiritual, ethical, literary, and political communication was in many ways a miniature medallion in which the very Rhodesian epic itself, with all of its unfulfilled possibilities, its tragedy and its promise, was tellingly mirrored.

The social sciences of our day whether in the political, sociological, or anthropological areas, are both intrigued and baffled in trying to fathom the problem of how communication takes place between men of sharply different cultures. This problem is as much unsolved in the attempts to carry out well-intentioned experiments in development today as it was in the preceding colonial régimes. It also haunts the internal life of independent countries where sharply differing cultures impinge upon each other. There has been far too little sympathy and understanding shown in the social sciences for the role that the religious missionary, for all of his limitations, has played in this process of significant communication. The study of such an immensely contemporary life as that of Arthur Cripps might well be commended to help balance the budget.

If a man like Cripps was to be taken as a case study, it would be clear that his spiritual message struggled inevitably in the Rhodesian colonial setting with the rival political, social, economic, and military presences which he was able to recognize and to acknowledge were continuously bombarding and irradiating the conscious and the unconscious life of the Africans with whom he sought to communicate. But after acknowledging these presences, Cripps was neither prepared to regard them as unchangeable nor to capitulate to them. For Cripps saw that if he were to give up, lest he or the Christian Church lose its good name by being identified with the wrongs of a colonial régime, or if he were to accommodate himself prudently to the existing régime, he would leave his own culture to make its impact upon the residents of Rhodesia largely devoid of the spiritual core which, for all of its infidelities, was nevertheless continually operating in his homeland to judge public conduct: to lift, to rebuke, to quicken its compassion, and to cut away the limits that it is always putting upon its liability for the well-being of *all* the people that it governs.

To have a spiritual emissary who was so sensitive to and so gifted in the deepest religious, aesthetic, and ethical insights of his own home country and yet who was open as well to the indigenous spiritual message that was already present and at work in the people of another culture and pattern of life among whom he came, meant that a remarkably favourable situation was set up for communication. Cripps seems to have had this quality in his life, for in spite of all of its falterings, there breathes a power and perhaps a message that could we fathom it, might throw real light on the whole dilemma of cross-cultural communication. It might also restore our confidence that even one man's faithfulness does not leave history unaffected.

Cripps was not only caught in the cross-currents of the rival resident presences that he faced in his half-century of living in Rhodesia. As a poet—and he is generally acknowledged as Rhodesia's greatest poet in his generation—he housed a fair-sized cross-fire within himself between the calling to write and his vocation as a missionary.

Cripps's acute sense of failure that dogged him from one end of his adult life to the other was certainly accentuated by the pain of living in this tension and by the relentless inner demand of each of these vocations. He thought that for the moment, at least, he had cut the knot when he made his original decision to leave Britain for Rhodesia. But hardly a day went by in Rhodesia that he did not, in spite of the exacting demands of his missionary duties, set down some lines of poetry or some pages of a manuscript. Henri Bremond in his *Prayer and Poetry* speaks of this secret cleft in the poet between his surveying the scene and his readiness for the oblivion of immersion as mystic-prophet. He uses a quaint figure of two persons in a wilderness coming upon a pool of incredible beauty. The poet at once withdraws to set down a description of his feelings upon the occasion of this ravishing encounter. The mystic-prophet, without the slightest hesitation, plunges into the very pool itself.

Cripps knew all too well the impulse to withdraw and to set down; he also knew the moments of complete immersion. Did he betray these moments in order to depict their shimmer? There were bold attempts in Cripps to preach his Keatsian gospel that truth and beauty are one and that the conflict between them is imaginary. There were patches when the poetic gifts that were threatened by the missionary vocation seem to have been restored to him for use in its service. But the stark setting of the tawdry pioneer dorp of Enkeldoorn to which he was chained, and the fierce spiritual and material needs, the Lazarus-like poverty of the African community to which he had given himself had a way of breaking through both his own constructions and the disclosures that faith had brought him and mocked all of his best efforts at their reconciliation. The figure of the One to whom he was devoted, nailed to a cross, had a stripping effect as he confronted it in the Daily Offices, and left him once again 'defenceless utterly'. Perhaps Unamuno in the closing line of his *The Tragic Sense of Life* could approach Cripps's situation when he wrote, 'May God deny you peace, but give you glory!' It must be confessed that Cripps felt the denial of peace more often than the gift of glory.

Readers who have an interest in what has been called 'the missionary factor' as it operated in the skeins of Rhodesian history and those who are still puzzled over the priest-prophet role of a Christian emissary anywhere, but very especially in a colonial missionary situation, will also find in Cripps's life and career a documentary that depicts unflinchingly one decisive form of witness. It is possible to describe a cluster of missionary roles. In the African situation, should the missionary be the spiritual arm of the white 'civilizing' force? Should the missionary be the impartial chaplain to black and white alike and seek to conduct the religious life of the community on a spiritual level that is above the plane of the political and economic conflicts that are at work in both races? Or should the missionary be deeply identified with the politically voiceless indigenous people of the colony and be prepared to break caste and brave the wrath of his own countrymen in order to expose glaring injustices and to appeal to the consciences of the domestic colonials, as well as to the sense of trusteeship and responsibility in the hearts of the home community to set these matters right?

Cripps's contribution to the missionary factor in Rhodesia left no ambiguity about which of these three roles he had chosen, for it was in the service of the voiceless indigenous people that he poured out his life. A sizeable share of his poetry, a variety of tracts and

books, testimonies to Royal Commissions, and a vast correspondence with key figures in Britain that was channelled by skilful
hands into questions put from the floor of the House of Commons
and used in summoning and preparing delegations to the powerful officials of the Colonial Office were all a part of the sinews that
Cripps threw into his missionary calling.

Cripps's stirring life does not contain any model resolutions of
any of these problems. For as one clerical colleague remarked,
'There is only one Cripps, thank God', and his grappling with
them was violent, intensely personal, and inimitable. To the Church,
to the State, and to his local confrères, he did not fit in. Canon
Edgar Lloyd, one of his two most intimate friends over the years,
wrote him late in his life. 'There are the regulars and the irregulars
and only God can use them both.' Arthur Shearly Cripps was
indelibly marked as one of God's irregulars.

It has been a gift of Britain to the world that she encouraged
many of the best of her sons to sow themselves in the far parts of
the earth where they could share their own genius in remote places,
leaving it to Providence to count both the cost and the harvest.
Cripps was a strange and disturbing gift to give to Rhodesia. But
the country is not the same for having had him planted as a
dynamic seed in its ancient granite soil.

There are several sources of manuscript material that have been
drawn upon in this biography. Arthur Cripps had been approached
by Rhodesia's great archivist, V. Hiller, and had agreed to leave his
papers to the National Archive in Rhodesia located at Salisbury.
When I first visited the Archive in 1955, the Cripps legacy was still
stored in a small trunk in which it had apparently been brought
from Enkeldoorn. By 1964 this material had been ordered and
classified and letters referred to here that are drawn from it are
listed as (N.A.). Present in this collection, but not arranged with
the others, is a special group of letters presented by Frank Mussels
and mainly containing letters which Cripps had sent to John White.
Letters from this collection have been labelled (J.W.). In addition
there is a collection of Cripps's correspondence which the late Archbishop Paget has loaned to the National Archive that is referred
to here as (P.C.). There is a small sheaf of letters mainly from
Cripps to H. Maynard Smith which is in the Godlingdon Collection in the University of Rhodesia Library that is marked here
(U.C.).

In England I was able to meet Elizabeth Cripps Roberts, who had by far the most important mass of Cripps material stored in her attic, and who was kind enough to entrust it to me for copying. This material has now been generously placed on loan in the archive of the Society for the Propagation of the Gospel in London and is the most valuable source that exists for the personal picture of Cripps. It is designated here as the Roberts Collection (R.C.). The files of the Anti-Slavery Society or what was more commonly called the Aborigines Protection Society were sold in 1962-3 to Rhodes House at Oxford and the letters up to 1940 are lodged there under the title, British Empire S 22, G 159-69. This is a treasure-trove of material to authenticate Cripps's political role from 1917-40 and is marked here as (A.P.S.).

The Fabian Colonial Bureau files for the period 1936-52 have also been used in several places, principally for the letters they contain of Arthur Creech-Jones. They are marked (F.C.B.). Much of the rest of the material has come from personal conversations in Rhodesia and Britain with those who knew Cripps and from memoranda and letters which they prepared for me. I have studied, as well, the Rhodesian newspapers and the Anglican periodicals and histories that cover the period of Cripps's active life, and the minute books of the Anglican Archives and the Rhodesian Missionary Society in Salisbury.

The kindness of innumerable persons who have helped me to assemble this material is almost beyond telling. In Rhodesia: Sir Robert and Lady Tredgold's friendship and encouragement; the help of Cecil William Alderson, the late Bishop of Mashonaland; the generous sharing of materials that she had assembled by Mrs Dorothy Finn, who has prepared an excellent study of Cripps's poetry; the gifts of time, of memoranda, of letters or of inscribed books given me by the late Archbishop Paget, Noel Brettell, Richard Nash, William Tully, Canon Christelow, the Reverend Richard Holderness, Canon Patterson, the Reverend John Stopford, the Reverend Anthony Deans Bailey, the late Reverend Oliver Roebuck, Mrs Wright, Mrs Comberback, Bessie Cullis, the Schultz family, the Reverend Frank Mussels, Dudley Robinson, and the most gracious archivists in Salisbury; the concerned visits that I was able to have with Cripps's African friends such as Leonard Mamvura, the late Reverend Cyprian Tambo, and Canon Edward Chipunza were all a witness to their caring for Cripps.

In England the Cripps family, Elizabeth and Douglas Roberts, Professor Hilary Armstrong (who has given permission for the use of the Cripps citations included in this volume), and Mrs Surrey Dane have all helped me in so many ways. Bess Pridmore, the archivist at the Society for the Propagation of the Gospel, went far beyond the bounds of duty to assist. In the matter of publication, I owe much to the Reverend Martin Jarret-Kerr, c.r., whose advice and continual ministrations have carried the bulk of the responsibility. The kindness of Norman Goodall, Eugene Exman, and of Professor Kenneth Kirkwood, Oxford Professor of Race Relations, in reading the manuscript and in making their helpful suggestions has been of invaluable assistance.

I want very especially to thank all of these persons, both named and unnamed, and to thank my wife and comrade, Dorothy, who shared this search with me and who has helped at every point in the preparation of the materials. I would once more express my gratitude to my faithful secretary, Mildred Hargreaves, whose skill in the final preparation of the manuscript was again put to use.

Haverford College   DOUGLAS V. STEERE
Haverford, Pa.
1 October 1971

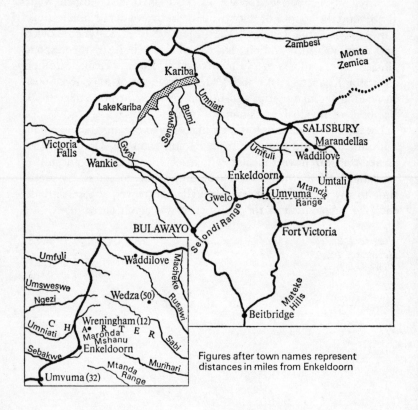

Figures after town names represent
distances in miles from Enkeldoorn

1

Oxford, Charles Gore, and a Decision

When Arthur Shearly Cripps matriculated at Trinity College, Oxford, in the autumn of 1887, he came into the charmed circle of English cultural life. An Oxford college could take whom it pleased, and it was not inclined to be overwhelmed by any of its candidates' distinctions, whether by reason of family or assembled evidence of youthful genius. There is a story of the President of Magdalen College writing to Japan a decade or two later about the admission of the Emperor's son, as a commoner at Magdalen, and of his assuring the Imperial Chamberlain that at Magdalen College, Chichibu, Son of God, would find himself in the company of the sons of many other distinguished gentlemen, and at least the flavour of relaxed arrogance in the tale is quite authentic. A future leading poet of Britain, future members of parliament, future bishops, scholars, and men of substance were all among Arthur Cripps's colleagues at Trinity College, for this was a particularly happy period in its long and rich life.

In admitting Arthur Shearly Cripps to the College, Trinity took a young man of good Kentish stock who had come up from Charterhouse School with a decent record and a reputation among his fellow students as a promising young poet. In fact, a slender volume of his verse had been privately published in 1884 when he was just fifteen that bore on its cover *A Selection of Poems*, by A. S. C., Tunbridge Wells, C. Bishop 'Gazette' Steam Printing Works. High Street, MDCCCLXXXIV. This may seem a little precocious, but with Laurence Binyon among the Trinity commoners of his time, Cripps's verse-making gifts would not want for company.

Cripps's family had not been much given to higher education. His grandfather, William Charles Cripps, had been a builder in Tunbridge Wells. Arthur Cripps's own father, another William

Charles Cripps, had been articled to a firm of solicitors and in 1852, when he was 21 years of age, had started a law firm of his own. In twenty years, by his own efforts, he had become not only the Town Clerk but also the Registrar and High Bailiff of the Tunbridge Wells Court.

In 1854, Arthur Cripps's father had married Catherine Charlotte Mary Shearly, the daughter of William Shearly, a London surgeon, and Arthur Shearly Cripps who was born on 10 June 1869 was the seventh of eight children, only four of whom lived to adulthood. The elder son, still another William Charles Cripps, was fifteen years older than his brother Arthur and had been pressed into the family law firm immediately after leaving Rugby. The third child, Edith Kate Cripps, who was some five years older than her brother, Arthur, and the eighth child, Emily Mary Cripps, who was four years younger, were the family companions with whom Arthur Cripps grew up.

Cripps himself did not believe that he was related to Sir Stafford Cripps, the British Chancellor of the Exchequer (1947-50). Lord Parmoor, who is today the head of the Cripps family to which Sir Stafford belonged, is less categorical. In a letter he wrote:

> As regards A. S. Cripps's relationship to my family, he may have been a distant cousin to whom our family records do not extend. He probably was, as there has been another branch of the family around Tunbridge Wells, which I believe dates back to a common ancestor very many years ago.

The career of Arthur Cripps's solicitor father was cut short by his sudden death in 1882 at the age of 51 when Arthur Cripps was 13 years old. From this time onward, the elder brother William became the head and financial guardian and guide of the family, and it was this brother who opened the way for Arthur to have the university training which he himself had been denied by the need for his early entry into the law firm of his father.

There is some evidence that Arthur Cripps went up to Oxford to get a grounding for the law. He actually corrected someone who late in his life spoke of his reading theology at Oxford by pointing out that he had been reading for the law, and his choice of the Honour School of Modern History after finishing his Moderations in the usual classical subjects would seem to bear this out.

It was not long before Cripps was in the full flood of an active career at Oxford. He worked his way to a seat in the first Trinity boat. He was a crack long-distance runner and shone in the three-mile races. He received his half-blue at Oxford in boxing. But physical sports were not to be all. Arthur Cripps is listed as the 151st member of the Oxford University Dramatic Society (OUDS). Alan Mackinnon's *Drama at Oxford* mentions Cripps in 1890 as playing the part of Willis, an adherent of Strafford, in Browning's *Strafford*, with Henry B. Irving, the son of England's immortal, in the title role.

The call to write poetry had not dimmed when Cripps left Charterhouse where he had few competitors. Instead it was greatly sharpened by his close friendship with Laurence Binyon, a friendship which lasted all his life and made a visit to the Binyons almost a fixture of every furlough-return to Britain. The *Oxford Magazine* in Cripps's undergraduate years carried poem after poem under the thinly disguised reversed initials of C. S. A. Writing in *The Scotsman* in November 1940, J. C. Smith recalls that he found in Oxford in 1888 a nest of singing birds:

> The best of whom was in my own college, Trinity. This was Laurence Binyon. In his second year having won the Newdigate [Poetry Prize] Binyon conspired with three other undergraduates to bring out a slim volume of verse *Primavera*. His collaborators were Ghose, the Indian poet, Arthur Shearly Cripps and Stephen Phillips. Cripps was a saint who spent his life in Mashonaland.

Primavera appeared in 1890 and won some favourable reviews.

From the very outset at Trinity, Cripps found himself in the hands of the college tutor in the ancient classics, R. W. Raper, who helped him to prepare for Classical Moderations which was a qualifying examination for the Honours School of Modern History. Here he experienced the one-teacher-one-student relationship of the regular weekly tutorials, an ideal which is realized at few places in the world apart from the senior English universities. Raper was able to guide Cripps in his classical studies and it was in his company that Cripps began his lifelong passion for Theocritus which had such a profound influence on his boundless appreciation for the African herdsmen and craftsmen who were to become his life companions.

R. W. Raper was one of those utterly dedicated celibate servants of his pupils and of his College who followed his men in their

careers as if they were his sons. Cripps sought his counsel on each of
the early moves that he made, and the relationship was so close
that it seemed quite natural for him to dedicate *Titania,* his own
first book of poems in his maturity, 'To R. W. Raper, Fellow of
Trinity College, Oxford, Gilt Verses in Return for Golden Inspira-
tions'. Fifteen years later, Cripps dedicated to him another volume
of poems, *Pilgrim's Joy,* which appeared when Cripps was a chaplain in the East African Campaign of what the Rhodesians call
'The Kaiser's War' just at the time of Raper's death, although Cripps
had not yet heard of it at the time.

Cripps read Modern History at Oxford and buried himself in the
fifteenth century which became his particular passion and which
was to furnish the setting for many of his entertaining stories. The
England of the Wars of the Roses seemed to engross him and few
have brought this age into life more vividly than Cripps was to do
in his collection of stories published under the title of *Magic Casements* and in many of his tales that appeared only in the magazines
of the day.

Arthur Cripps came up to Oxford with a vigorous High Church
Anglican bent that had been nurtured by the strong family ties with
St Barnabas church at Tunbridge Wells which was staunchly
Anglo-Catholic. At Charterhouse this had been tempered a little,
but at Oxford he soon came under the influence of Charles Gore,
who was then in his mid-thirties and at the height of his powers as
a spiritual leader of men. Gore, too, was a Trinity College man
and had from 1883 on been Principal of the new Pusey House
which was located in two remodelled private houses in St Giles
directly opposite St John's College. Five years later, when Cripps
was at Oxford, J. H. Adderley could write of it:

> Pusey House was to the Oxford of that day what St Mary's was
> to the Oxford of the days of Newman. Gore's influence was the
> greatest in Oxford since John Henry Newman's (J. H. Adderley,
> *Slums and Society,* London 1916, p. 11).

In addition to Charles Gore's extensive personal entertaining of
students at Pusey House there was the Saturday night service of
preparation for Holy Communion and the Sunday noon and Mon-
day evening 'voluntary lectures' given to some fifty or sixty under-
graduates. There he dealt with the Bible, theology, ethics, and the
social problems of the time. At the time of Charles Gore's death in

1932, Arthur Cripps wrote a poem, *Charles Gore at Oxford*, which gives some feeling of how, forty years later, he remembered the grip of this spiritual guide upon the hearts and minds of his generation. The poem describes Gore preaching at St Barnabas' church, a favourite place for those of Gore's persuasion:

> Whom went we forth—we boys of old—to hear?
> One with wan face, rough brows, and hermit's beard,
> A brooding preacher. How o'ercast and blear'd
> Were his encavern'd eyes, how slow to clear!
>
> How blindly groped his hands, as tho' they'd tear
> Pillars like fumbling Samson's! Ere it near'd
> Its cataracts—how cok'd his speech appear'd—
> A dull brook trickling thro' the marshlands drear!
>
> Then that light blaz'd at last, that Whirlwind blew:
> He bow'd himself before the o'rruling might
> Of driving gusts with furious lightnings bright;
> To a prophet's stature, while we gaz'd, he grew—
> Beside himself, possess'd by God anew—
> An oblate—ear to ground—on Horeb's height!

But the Gore who drew Cripps away from a career in the law and into the service of the Church was more than a brooding prophet with a scorching touch of the numinous about him. All of the spiritual and the social forces that swirled in Oxford and that did so much to tear the Oxford Movement free of its Tory associations and to broaden and deepen its witness seemed to have formed a rare amalgam in the Gore of this period, and it would be next to impossible to understand how Cripps was won to take Holy Orders without some grasp of their focus. J. H. Adderley put it well when he wrote:

He [Gore] fitted the Incarnation into the requirements of the new learning, and into the aspirations of the younger men to the solution of social problems ... the honey collected by Frederick Denison Maurice passed into the hive of the ritualists. ... A new type of high church parson was being fabricated at Pusey House and sent down to East London to explode like the shells in Flanders. Gore was the quiet old chemist thinking out ways of meeting unbelief and indifference (J. H. Adderley, op. cit., p.120).

The Christian Social Union, which Cripps promptly joined and to which he often refers, was organized in 1889 by Henry Scott Holland at St Paul's in London, but the Oxford Chapter was immediately initiated in Pusey House under Gore's encouragement. It sought to reach the man in the pew and from within the Church of England to convince its members of their unlimited liability for social conditions all about them. Student members of the C.S.U. at Oxford organized and published lists of local employers who paid their workers sub-union wages; hunted out acts of neglect of proper safeguards of workers exposed to lead poisoning or to unguarded machines; campaigned against sweated conditions in industries employing female labour; and urged programmes of public works in forests and on public lands in order to give gainful work to the unemployed.

When, in August 1889, the Dock Strike broke out in London, Henry Scott Holland from his powerful post in St Paul's succeeded in bringing both Charles Gore from Oxford and the Bishop of London into conference, and together, these three Christian leaders were no small force in pressing the Establishment into acknowledging the justice of the workers' demands for a raise in wages from fourpence to sixpence an hour! 'Gore and Holland tried to win authority to their side and claim for Christian law the ultimate authority to rule Christian practice' (Maurice Reckitt, *From Maurice to Temple* London 1949, p.38).

For Arthur Cripps, this accent on the Christian social witness was decisive, and Charles Gore had taken away his fear of either intellectual obscurantism or of social or ethical irrelevancy on the part of the Church, and yet had kept the centrality of the Sacraments and of the givenness of the Christian religion. It is pure speculation, but there are hints that Arthur Cripps's commitment to the life of celibacy was profoundly strengthened by the example of Charles Gore and Henry Scott Holland as well as by his friend-to-come, J. H. Adderley. The Oxford Movement in restoring the Catholic tradition in the Church of England had always included a genuine ascetical and even penitential element. It was, therefore, quite natural to find Charles Gore in this same momentous year of 1889 quietly taking the first steps towards founding the Community of the Resurrection, a monastic order whose members were to be utterly expendable in the service of the Anglican Church.

It may seem a curious thing that Gore, while the Founder of the

Community of the Resurrection and a lifetime admirer and sup-
porter of its role in the Anglican Church, never felt called to bind
himself to its corporate monastic life. Here again Cripps found
in Gore a kindred spirit. For while Cripps was later to discover in
this very Community of the Resurrection's Rhodesian centre at Penhalonga a citadel of strength for the missionary witness of the
Church, he knew from the outset that it was not for him. There was
a sense in which Gore and Cripps were essentially unregimentable
and would have found almost unbearable any corporate stifling of
the prophetic fire which both seemed marked to give. Even as a
bishop in the Church of England, Gore could blaze out, 'I hate
the Church of England: an ingeniously devised instrumentality to
defeat the objects it was meant to promote', and Cripps was even to
refuse to be licensed by the Church of South Africa in the closing
years of his career.

Yet for both it was so clearly a lover's quarrel. Neither relented
for a moment in the limitless self-giving that his commitment asked
of him. Both knew well enough what Bishop Creighton meant
when, in a letter to J. H. Adderley, he wrote, 'The world will be
moved by seeing a spirit not its own, and this spirit must never
work in the world's way'. But for both men the discipline and the
asceticism which they espoused had to be self-imposed. Both seemed
destined to follow out their consciences wherever these might lead
them and to hang on to the concern that had come to them with a
stubbornness and a tenacity that only the company of the prophets
can ever understand. Both were willing to let the chips fall where
they would and to show little sign of being smoothly meshed with
their fellows. It is not surprising, then, that Cripps found in
Charles Gore one who rolled away the stone and who, before his
Oxford days were over, opened the way for him to prepare himself
to enter the ministry of the Church of England.

2

Adderley, St Francis, and a
Call to Rhodesia

In the summer of 1891 Cripps took his B.A. in Modern History with second-class honours. Although he had by this time made up his mind to take orders in the Church of England, he still had the whole of his theological preparation before him. For this he went to Cuddesdon, a small and rather intimate Anglican seminary some twelve miles from Oxford. It had been called into being by the Bishop of Oxford some thirty years before in order to try to remedy Oxford University's own over-academic training for the clergy, and to provide a place where the Church's sacramental and corporate worship could be cultivated during the time when the men were reading for the theological examinations which candidates for Holy Orders were required to pass.

At the close of this year of theology, Cripps, as the most distinguished student of his class, was chosen to be Gospeller at the Ordination service at which he was made a deacon in July 1892 by the Bishop of Chichester. He received his first appointment as an assistant curate at Icklesham in Sussex. A year later he was ordained priest by the same bishop, W. E. Russell.

In the meanwhile the Tunbridge Wells home had been given up by his mother and his two sisters, Edith and Emily Mary, and the family had gone to live in a house in Torquay in Devonshire. A little over a year after his father's death in 1882, his beloved mother, Charlotte Cripps, had been secretly received into the Roman Catholic Church, and five years later Edith had joined her. The move to Torquay meant that mother and daughters could be closely associated with a French order of teaching nuns called the Daughters of the Cross, who conducted a small school for girls in Torquay. By the end of the century, his mother and Edith moved into an apartment in the school itself and lived there most happily as guests of the nuns for the rest of their lives. During this time Emily Mary Cripps had married the Reverend W. Armstrong, a High Church Tory Anglican curate whom she had known at St Barnabas' church in Tunbridge Wells where he had served. His violent disapproval of the Roman Catholic connection of his sister-in-law, Edith, seems to have walled her away from them, but Charlotte Cripps, his saintly mother-in-law, was irresistible, and her fondness for him managed to keep her tie with the Armstrong family happily strong as long as she lived. One of Arthur Cripps's Armstrong nieces remembers with what delight they looked forward to her grandmother Charlotte Cripps's visits and of how she always provided surprises in the way of little presents and had once taken her out and bought her her first meringue!

In 1894, Arthur Cripps, now a priest with some modest season-ing in his Sussex curacy, was given his first independent post as a vicar. The church was at Ford End in Essex, some thirty-five miles north-east of London. It was a Trinity College living, and as the times went, it was an excellent appointment with a stipend of £350 a year, a large rectory, and religious duties which did not over-tax him and which seemed especially suited for an incumbent who was inclined to literary pursuits.

Cripps was now immersed in a truly rural situation, and he was soon made captive both by the charm of Essex, as his later poetry will indicate, and by the rhythm of the seasons which only country folk may truly know. In the large, austere, nineteenth-century brick church at Ford End, his services were dignified. He soon found that his parishioners were not at home with the High Church liturgy to which he was accustomed; he bent to their taste and within the limits of his deep reverence for the Sacrament, he did little to offend them. His reading of the liturgy and of the Scrip-tures is reported as both bold and beautiful, and his preaching unbelievably simple, brief, and to the point. A local man who is still alive remembers his religious instruction in the village school at Ford End, as remarkably clear, and something that you did not forget.

Cripps extended his parish duties by establishing a small mission church at Littley Green some two miles away. By his amazing stamina as a runner he managed to conduct a service there, and then to trot back to Ford End in time for the regular service. He was an indefatigable visitor of the sick and apparently thought nothing of jogging the sixteen-mile return journey to Chelmsford to visit one of his flock in the hospital. There was always a stick of chocolate for the patient or some other little gift that he had brought along.

He was sympathetic with Henry George and with his attempts to preserve for the community any gains in the value of land by his ingenious schemes of taxation. Cripps also was keenly interested in the preservation of the village commons and was devoted to the movement that sought to recover these commons for the people to use as their own. He readily offered the church green to the villagers for use in Morris dancing.

Cripps had been at Ford End for scarcely a year when he met the Reverend J. H. Adderley at a clergy conference at Stebbing in Essex, and he was one of the vicars who invited Adderley to conduct a religious mission in his parish. This was the beginning of a friendship that was to continue and to deepen in him the work which Gore and Scott Holland had begun in the Oxford days. At the time of Adderley's death in 1941 he wrote:

A good companion, a beloved vagabond. But he had a much higher command on my respect and affection. He was the Friend of God's Poor. Were there not often, even in the golden days of Queen Victoria, many unfriended or comparatively unfriended, poor in Essex country parishes? It was when he was seeking to befriend these, that I first met James Adderley (Arthur Shearly Cripps, *Memoir of James H. Adderley* (unpublished), National Archives, Salisbury, Rhodesia).

Arthur Cripps was often with Adderley in the years between 1895 and 1900 and they became fast companions. Cripps, in this unpublished manuscript on J. H. Adderley, describes one of the many mission trips they took together:

On Tuesday in Whitsun week 1896, we started from where Adderley had a Home for Lay Brothers at the time. He was the head of the Society for the Divine Compassion and wore its habit. We were to go in faith asking help for our way, as early evangelists may have gone. My rather crazy notion of walking barefoot with unproved feet was overruled, and I walked in sandals. We went by Barkingside and Havering to Brentwood, where we slept the night. We went to the dosshouse, where we

had singing in the kitchen that evening, but we slept in a sort
of an annexe next door. My companion confided to me next
day that he had found fellow creatures as bedfellows, passive if
not active. We reached the village of our mission that day...
We had a platform for preaching from the village green. Adderley in those day edited *Good Will*, a spiritual parish magazine.
I remember a passage in its account of our mission which ran
like this: 'When parson Cripps was preaching, one could see
his corduroys under his cassock. He looks a guy, and so do I'.
After a Sunday service I remember producing a clay pipe from
my pocket when I was in the company of the village publican,
making some kind of apology about smoking cheap tobacco
and for indulging in a luxury like smoking. His answer gave
me no quarter and I honour him for it (ibid.).

There were many other such journeys where they interspersed
train and walking and dossing. When they went through villages,
there was great amusement at their Anglo-Catholic get-up, and
Adderley loved the workmen's fun-poking queries just as he did
the heckling at the open-air speaking stands. 'Ees got me awld
wife's night-gownd on', or 'Whin air they goin to burn ye?' 'Ees
got a rope to 'ang 'isself with', or 'Did you iver see sich a curi-
ousity outside of Oirland?' It was Adderley who preached for
Cripps at the Harvest Festival in Ford End in 1900 just before he
left Essex for Rhodesia, and it was to Adderley, now settled at
Saltley in Birmingham, where his revolutionary influence continued, that Cripps went for a stay in 1906 'before my first long
leave from Africa ended'.

In 1942, thinking back over his friend's eighty years in which
he remained as fresh as a boy until the very end, Cripps wrote,
'He was surely a pioneer, a burning and a shining light of the
school of St John the Baptist'. It would be hard to overestimate
the influence which this revolutionary fellow-Franciscan, James
Adderley, exerted on the life-style of both Arthur Cripps and
Bishop Frank Weston.

During the last two years (1898-1900) of his first term at Ford
End, Arthur Cripps served as one of the Poor Law Guardians.
He took a deep interest in the tramps and their hardships. He and
a fellow Guardian were able to get one unnecessary local aggrava-
tion changed in 1900, so that it was no longer necessary for the

tramps to make the long journey from the poorhouse casual
ward to the town and back again in order to get and to present a
certificate authorizing a meal and a night's lodging. He wrote of
these experiences in a Christmas poem which he called *The
Vagrant's Carol*, which appeared in *Titania*, London 1900, pp.34-5.

God, whose love at Christmas on our lost world smiled,
Speed the tired child travellers through this winter wild,
He at thy right hand in heaven was an outcast's child.

Jesus, thou that hadst not where to lay thy head,
Care for these that wander, sheep unshepherded,
Count each needless step men send them, homeless and unfed!

Christ, it is thy birthday, cold the winds to-day,
Rise and shine the sterner cold of Christian hearts away,
Thou the Vagrant-Mother's Child she cradled in the hay.

Two other poems of moderate length record the depth of these
experiences for him. In *At the Shrine of St Vincent de Paul* (ibid.,
p.57), the seventeenth-century French apostle to the poor, he closes
with,

O thou that caredst for each brute's dull face
In all thy drove, and for one convict's moan
Would'st leave a ninety-nine of burghers just,

Pray for my heart and all poor hearts of stone,
That we may render grace for Jesu's grace,
And love as thou didst love our fellow dust.

In *London's Litany of the Saints* (ibid., p.61), one of his eight
petitions is directed to St Joseph and reads:

Pray for the men who loaf and lie,
Pray for the men who curse and die,
Pray for the men who sleep in the cold,
Pray for God's Image, bought cheap and sold,
Patron of men necessitous!

.   .   .   .

Joseph of Bethlehem, pray for us!

The little volume *Titania* in which these three poems are found
was largely written between the years of 1898 and 1900 while Cripps

was shepherding his small Essex flock, feeding, preaching, visiting, marrying, and burying, well interspersed with occasions of missionizing and dossing. We have little else to help us but his poems for what took place in these critical years as he crossed the theshold into his thirties. That he adored Essex and loved every tree and stone and hedge and field with an almost pagan passion was more than clear. That he had a small circle of Oxford and London friends and his own close family who cherished him is evident as well. There is later evidence that at this time he was already at work on short stories and novels where his romantic bent and his historical fervour could have sway.

In the long poem 'The Death of St Francis' which some regard as the richest nugget in the *Titania* collection and a large section of which is quoted in the *Oxford Book of Mystical Verse,* there seem to be flashes of telling self-disclosure that are as near to autobiography as we shall ever get. This poem gives a moving description of the dying Francis trying to tell his brethren what really happened to him in the wild and lonely thicket of Alverna where Francis's own body and limbs were marked with the Stigmata, the five wounds of Christ's passion:

> How can I tell it? The thing is sacred, dear...
> Hands grew to hands, feet seemed to grow to feet,
> His hands to my hands, feet of his to mine;
> Exalted and extended on his cross,
> I seemed in one great stab of eager pain
> To feel his heart beating within my heart...
> It seemed he lent his Sacred Heart to me:
> One moment did I know his wish, his work,
> As if mine own they were, and knew with them
> The worm-like weakness of my wasted life,
> My service worthless to win back his world....
>
> I knew in blissful anguish what it means
> To be a part of Christ, and feel as mine
> The dark distresses of my brother limbs,
> To feel it bodily and simply true,
> To feel as mine the starving of his poor....'

It is hard to believe that this poem, coming as it does with Cripps turned thirty, at the height of his powers as a poet, and at a major fork of decision in the road of his religious commitment, is not to be taken as a clue to the struggle that was going on behind the façade of this well-established Essex parish priest. The note of the sense of failure that haunted him all his life is unmistakeable. Especially significant are his words: 'The worm-like weakness of my wasted life. My service worthless to win back his world'. Neither as a poet nor as a priest had Cripps really laid hold of the world. Both callings taunt him with his failure. But from what ground within him have these reproaches come? Are they from the shattering of the secret neurotic strategy of his own heart? Had he somehow contrived to furnish himself with a way of escape like C. P. Snow's Lewis Eliot, the lawyer, who divided himself between his London practice and a law fellowship at a Cambridge college in order to assure himself that, should he never reach the highest round in either place, he might have done so but for his faithfulness to both London and Cambridge? Or are they from the eternal war between the aesthetic and the religious stages or intensities of life which Søren Kierkegaard has so brilliantly depicted? Or is the reproach of failure simply the shadow cast by the blaze of love that he has known which makes any human performance fall infinitely short of its supreme inviting? Or may all three clefts have found a place in him?

Certainly for Cripps, the image of the Five Wounds and of the Compassionate Heart that beats within his own was to colour and to go on shaping the fifty years of life that remained to him, and the Franciscan mark of *disponibilité* in the service of this passion was burned into him like a rancher's brand which nothing can ever remove. But healed scars, too, have a way of reopening and of vindicating the wisdom of the Church's ancient insistence that, even for the best of men, there is in this life no early retirement on a life annuity, but only a path that leads 'up-hill all the way, yes, to the very end'.

What was it that really led Cripps, who, in spite of these depreciations, was already well on the stair of a career as a gifted poet-priest, a Victorian George Herbert with an even more moving Franciscan flair, to turn away from the England that he loved, to resign his good Ford End living, and at the age of 31 to set out late in 1900 for Mashonaland in Rhodesia as a missionary of the Society for the Propagation of the Gospel? Who will ever know?

His own deep dissatisfaction with his life as poet and priest in the Essex setting has been indicated. Should he give himself to a more caring and costly enterprise, to one that might even blot out the call to serve the muse in favour of the call to serve God's poor? In 1898, his brilliant Trinity College friend, Frank Weston, who was later to become bishop of Zanzibar and who, like Cripps, had fallen under the spell of Adderley and, through him, of the Christ of the poor, had cut the knot and taken a mission post almost on the equator in the Zanzibar and East Africa region. This decision of Frank Weston's could not have been lost on Arthur Cripps.

In 1897, the South African Boer writer, Olive Schreiner, who fifteen years before had fascinated the British literary world with her *Story of an African Farm,* published a political tract in the form of a melodramatic novel, *Trooper Peter Halket of Mashona-land.* She had written it swiftly in the white heat of fury after the Jameson Raid in 1895, the abortive coup by which Rhodes's colleague, Dr Jameson, had tried in vain to topple the Boer leader, Paul Kruger, from power in the Transvaal, and during the time of the harsh white Rhodesian suppression of the Matabele and Mashona rebellions that began in 1896. The book was a scathing attack on Cecil Rhodes, on his Chartered Company, and on the whole Rhodesian enterprise which Rhodes had supported out of his fabulous wealth. The frontispiece of the book consisted of a gruesome reproduction of a photograph of the swinging bodies of three African captives who had been strung up to the branches of a mimosa tree, as an example of what would happen to traitorous leaders, by a small band of white Rhodesians who are shown lounging about complacently as though they were well satisfied with a good morning's work.

The story of the book depicts the acts of the Rhodesian Ahab, Cecil J. Rhodes, in seizing the vineyard of the poor black Naboth. In the concluding scene, Trooper Peter Halket's ruthless Rhodesian captain, in order to pay Peter off for his humane feelings for a tortured African captive, orders him to shoot the captive at dawn. Trooper Peter liberates the captive and is himself executed.

Arthur Cripps in England read this book some three years later and was deeply moved by it. He told his godson, William Tully, that it was reading Olive Schreiner's *Trooper Peter Halket of Mashonaland* with its horrible frontispiece that had touched off in

him a determination to place a few years of his own life in the
scale-pan on the side of the African, and to try in some small way
to lessen the accumulated weight of wrong which his own people
had done to them. Perhaps he might assist in some way in convincing his black brethren that there was One at the heart of
things who cared utterly for them. 'One moment did I know his
wish, his work, as if mine own they were.'

The implementing of this decision was a matter of a few months.
There is an undocumented but persistent rumour of a love affair
with a girl which might have changed Cripps's earlier drawing
towards the celibate life. This was apparently terminated by the
decision for Africa. There are poems written on the journey out
which fit convincingly into such a surmise.

Cripps offered himself to the Anglican missionary body, The
Society for the Propagation of the Gospel (familiarly known in
Cripps's day as SPG and now as USPG), which was already supporting the Anglican work in Rhodesia, and was accepted. He
resigned his living at Ford End, a step to which R. W. Raper, his
old Trinity College tutor, had finally given his reluctant assent.
His elder brother, William, who had the task of winding up his
final affairs in Essex, had pressed him to limit his promise for this
mission work to a term of two years, and to this Arthur Cripps
had consented. He refers in a poem to his expected return to
England when he has fulfilled his 'vow'.

The normal and most simple route to Rhodesia would have been
by ship to Cape Town and then by rail to Bulawayo in Rhodesia.
But the Boer War was now in its full fury and rail passage through
South Africa quite impossible. He therefore secured a berth on a
German passenger vessel, the *Hertzog*, which travelled through the
Suez Canal and then down the east coast of Africa to the port of
Beira in Mozambique which would permit Cripps to enter Rhod-
esia through the back door and to cross into this landlocked
territory just east of Umtali.

Cripps's book of poems *Titania*, which is full of Keatsian lyrics
and reveals not only his religious bent but something of the broad
humanity of his affections, was published in London shortly before
he left, but the reviews were slow in coming. He was therefore
on his way to Africa before the verdict of his peers was registered
on this collection into which he had poured the best that these post-
Oxford years had enabled him to create. He left England in a

state of suspense. While he had now turned his back on the muse, he was not above the temptation to see how others regarded the promise in that which he had renounced.

3

Rhodesia in 1901:
the Apprenticeship

The time of Cripps's departure for Rhodesia had come. After a handsome farewell dinner given him in London by his friend and college contemporary, Laurence Binyon, at which there was a reading of Binyon's poem, *Death of Tristram*, Cripps spent a night at Tunbridge Wells with his lawyer brother, William, who showered him with an older brother's advice and counsel. Writing to Charlotte Cripps, William reported:

> We got him a comfortable carriage ... and I gave him a pound of good tobacco as I found he had none ... I gave him £12. ....
> I impressed upon him that this money was for his personal use and that he would be committing a breach of trust if he expended it either on church matters or charity ... He has promised me faithfully to write you every mail and to make no engagement whatever binding himself for more than two years until after he has been at home at the end of that period ... He is a real good fellow—too good in fact and too impractical just at present to cope with the world (1 December 1900).

(The letters which are cited in Chapters 3-7, unless otherwise designated, are from the Elizabeth Roberts' Collection, which is now on loan to the USPG library in London.)

Arthur Cripps, who was an inveterate pipe-smoker, may have found that he valued this pound of 'the herb most kind' even more highly than his solicitous elder brother's counsel and his judgement of his unfitness for the rugged new world that he was on his way to enter.

From Rome he wrote to his younger sister, Emily Mary, about his farewell from the church at Ford End: 'The people came out so well in the end ... which was the sort of God-speed I really valued. I found out how really fond of them I was at the last' (3 December 1900). Rome was for him a 'torrent of grandeur' but it was the graves of Shelley and of Keats that seemed to touch him most. He joined the *Hertzog* at Naples.

The long sea journey southwards on a vessel which called at most of the ports gave him time to write some fresh poems and the ship's double stop at Zanzibar made possible a three-day visit with his beloved Trinity College friend, Frank Weston, later bishop of Zanzibar, whose Franciscan bent matched his own.

Arthur Cripps's future costume emerges in a note to his mother:

I got a khaki suit off an Arab yesterday: it was only four shillings: I think a friend, a third-class passenger is going to sew on the trouser buttons strongly and then it will be very serviceable for me.

His characteristic concern as a spokesman for the needs and rights of others appears in the same letter:

I went to the captain about the drippy and wretched state of some of the native deck passengers ... He said he would see about it, and to my great joy he seems to have inspected the place and screened them from the weather comfortably (30 December 1900).

The next episode, however, did not end so amicably, and even before he left the ship, he managed to plunge himself into the world of which he had chosen to become a part. While Cripps was still asleep early on the morning of 3 January 1901, the *Hertzog* arrived at Beira Bay, the principal port of Portuguese Mozambique, and proceeded to prepare the African Somali deck passengers for transfer to shore where, as a labour corps for work on rail construction, they were to be taken by rail to Rhodesia. Cripps describes the incident in a letter:

We took a lot of Somali aboard at Aden, who were to work on the Rhodesian railway. Apparently the Germans [aboard the *Hertzog*] made them believe they would be treated as slaves or would be badly paid, and they refused to come ashore, and knocked a Portuguese policeman about rather badly, perhaps seriously. This row occurred about 5 or 6 in the day we came into port ... to my bitter sorrow I knew nothing of the row

pending, went to bed early, and slept through it all. The Roman
Father who saw it told me it was a horrible scene. The Portuguese
rushed these people with drawn swords and tried to bundle them
into a barge. Two were killed and ten I think were reported
missing. The Englishman I am staying with says that the two
dead had shot wounds ... two more bodies have been washed
up. A Scotch captain picked up 7 or so almost dead-beat who had
swam away and he refused to deliver them to the Portuguese.
If the *Hertzog*'s captain had only stood firm and refused to allow
his men to be shifted till morning, they might have gone quietly.
I did feel a beast having slept through it ... Some of the English
feel genuinely indignant; then there is the natural antipathy
against the Portuguese, and also the natural feeling about the
scare likely to be created in the labour market. It is a characteristic sort of introduction, I fear, to this dark continent (5 January
1901).

It would be hard to imagine a more startling way to let Arthur
Cripps begin to experience inwardly a whole range of elements
of the Rhodesian world he was entering. In the first place this
rancid, sweltering Portuguese port of Beira where he had landed
was Rhodesia's only maritime port of entry and exit for the whole
Northern and Eastern regions of her territory. Salisbury, Rhodesia's
capital, was 370 miles west and a little north of Beira, but it was
1700 miles north and east of the only other great seaport, Cape
Town, 'with the final Cape Town railway link covering the two-
hundred-and-fifty-mile stretch from Bulawayo to Salisbury still a
year from completion at this time.

In the harsh struggle in 1890 and 1891, Cecil Rhodes's Charter
Company constabulary and a small detail of troops had taken
matters into their own hands and put the Portuguese forces to
rout, made treaties with the African Paramount Chiefs, and been
only two days' march from Beira and the securing for Rhodesia,
once and for all, of this vitally important two-hundred-mile-long
corridor from Rhodesian Umtali to the Indian Ocean. However,
the long-delayed Portuguese signing of Lord Salisbury's British-
Portuguese treaty covering the boundaries between Mozambique,
Nyasaland, Barotseland, and Rhodesia intervened and the Rhodesian forces were ordered by British authority to turn back. To
Rhodes's bitter disappointment, this Rhodesian free-way to the sea

was restored to Portuguese hands where it has remained ever since.

Portugal, after centuries of neglect, had in the flurry of the great powers' lust for colonies, laid claim not only to the 'saddle-bags' of Mozambique and Angola (Portuguese East and West Africa) but to the whole vast Central African 'saddle' that lay between them, and Spain and France were content to acknowledge these claims in their 1886 treaties with Portugal. Rhodes in Cape Town, with his telescopic eye focused northward upon Cairo and the ultimate British control of a Cape-to-Cairo axis, was contemptuous of these Portuguese claims and was determined that Britain should possess the 'Saddle'. His real answer to the Portuguese was to have his emissaries deal directly with the effective Paramount Chief of the Central African area, Lobengula, and to secure the Rudd Concession in 1888, granting to Rhodes's group the right to extract metals from this territory and the necessary authority to carry this out. He next secured, in 1889, a British Charter for a Chartered Company modelled on the East India Company with a vast authority to rule the territory. The members of Rhodes's column which established effective British occupation in 1890, were the pioneers of a stream of white immigrants into the country, bent on mining for gold and eventually on ranching and cattle raising. The two huge regions that made up the Rhodesian territory had originally been called Matabeleland (Southern and Western region) and Mashonaland (Northern and Eastern region) after the principal African tribes who occupied them. But by 1895, at Dr Jameson's suggestion these both became known as Rhodesia, taking the name of the visionary who had charted their course.

This incident aboard the *Hertzog* was also to give Arthur Cripps a glimpse into the African labour situation in Rhodesia and the desperate stake of the white community in the extension of the railways as their life-line of supplies and communication. For the Somalis who were involved in this ugly affair were being brought into Rhodesia as an African substitute for the local Mashona labour that, as Cripps would soon discover, did not surge forward to the white settler's call either to work his farms, to mine his gold, or to build his railways. The Charter Company had both borrowed and used its own capital lavishly to finance these railways. In 1897 Bulawayo had been linked by rail with Cape Town in South Africa and the cost of transporting indispensable supplies from the

Cape, while still high, had dropped from £70 to £10 a ton. The narrow-gauge Rhodesian-built railway on which Cripps was to travel from Beira to Umtali had still to be linked to a broader gauge line from Umtali to Salisbury, and from Salisbury to Bulawayo, to say nothing of the western and north-western rail arms to reach the coal at Wankie, to connect Livingstone, and ultimately to go as far as the vast metal-mining areas of Broken Hill. But Charter Company money drawn from the pockets of British people had to be linked with the backs of strong and willing labourers to provide this highway of steel for the new territory, and Cripps would soon discover that here was a focus of African-White friction with which he would be struggling throughout his whole ministry in Rhodesia.

The Bishop of Mashonaland was at Beira to meet the ship and to welcome this unusual poet-missionary to his labours. Bishop William Gaul was barely five feet tall and claimed he was 'the smallest Bishop with the largest diocese in Christendom'. He was a man's man who had come up to Rhodesia in 1895 from the South African diamond capital of Kimberley, where he was both rector and archdeacon, in order to carry on the killing work of a pioneer bishop. As bishop he was charged with nothing short of the establishing of the Anglican Church in this huge domain and the carrying of the Christian message to a million Africans.

His predecessor, the distinguished Bishop George W. H. Knight-Bruce, when he was still the youngest bishop ever to be appointed to Blomfontein, had made a three-thousand-mile trek of exploration into the Mashonaland area of Central Africa in 1888, walking a good part of the way. The Congregationalist London Missionary Society was already at work in Matabeleland and the Universities Mission to Central Africa was active to the north in Nyasaland. Bishop Knight-Bruce was determined to find out if Mashonaland, the territory between these two regions, was a place which the Anglican Church had a responsibility to missionize, and if the way seemed open for this venture, to seek to establish friendships with as many chiefs as he could visit, in order to prepare for the coming of the Church. With no roads, the ever-present malaria and the tse-tse fly belts which prevented the passage of either horses or oxen for transport; with lions, elephants, and all kinds of wild beasts plentiful; with food, apart from what you could shoot, almost unprocurable and carriers most reluctant to leave their local

areas; and with the general attitude of the Africans highly uncertain; the journey was a stiff one. He returned, however, in
1889, and recommended the establishment of a chain of Anglican
missions between Bechuanaland and the Zambesi River.

In 1889 Knight-Bruce resigned his secure Blomfontein bishopric
and at the age of thirty-nine accepted his election as the first bishop
of 'Mashonaland and Adjacent Territories'. In 1891 he entered
Rhodesia through the port of Beira. Rhodes's pioneer column had
opened up the territory a year before and in their number Bishop
Knight-Bruce had sent three of his clergy, although one of them
had died within a matter of months after his arrival in Salisbury.
Between May and October in 1891, the new Bishop, in spite of
constant malaria, managed to walk 1,300 miles through his new
diocese. Bishop Knight-Bruce lasted a bare three years before he
was invalided to England with blackwater fever. His health was
so broken that he died of fever and pneumonia at the age of 44.
William Gaul succeeded him.

Peppery little Bishop Gaul was a tough and sprightly figure
dressed in a khaki drill apron in addition to a khaki clerical coat
and a helmet. His diminutive size could, however, be misinterpreted,
as a rough and tipsy miner, riding in a railway coach, once discovered when the Bishop warned him that if he did not stop his
obscene language he would be put off the coach. The miner turned
on the Bishop belligerently and boasted, 'If you wasn't a sky pilot,
I'd knock the stuffing out of you!' The Bishop whipped off his
apron, rolled his shirt sleeves to the elbows, and squared up to the
man. 'There's the Bishop of Mashonaland', he said, pointing to
his discarded garments, 'and here's Billy Gaul. Now come on'
(ibid, p.23).

Arthur Cripps, who stood a vigorous five-foot-ten-inches of lean
muscle, and held an Oxford half-blue in boxing, was not exactly
an effeminate type, but he had little in his background to prepare
him for the rough settler type of white man that he was to meet in
Rhodesia. Even Bishop Gaul, with a generation of diamond diggers
in Kimberley to knock about and manage, and an easy rough-and-
ready way with every human type, was one before whom Cripps
thawed slowly. Cripps wrote his mother:

The Bishop is a real good sort in his way. Between ourselves I
am a little doubtful about the peculiar khaki tinge of the type of

priestcraft that is in front of me, but I am quite ready to be fair and sympathetic to it, so help me God (undated but January 1901).

Cripps, who had stayed in Beira with his Anglican brethren of the Universities Mission to Central Africa, was and always remained a devoted sacramentalist, but he was quietly critical of their ecclesiastical firmnesses of form in the thrust of the mission field. Yet he deeply admired these UMCA priests and he knew the utter devotion with which they gave themselves to the African, regardless of the cost. The missionary, François Coillard's, remark that 'We have taken possession of the country by our graves' was no exaggeration, and Patrick Keatley writes that 'For the men of the missions, from the time they set foot on Rhodesian soil, there was a scant five years before death or invaliding home'. It was customary for a new recruit to make a will and choose a word for his headstone, though he might be under thirty and perfectly fit. The UMCA reported at the turn of the century that out of 200 men who had come to their missions 57 had died in service. There could be little doubt that Cripps was joining an expendable profession.

The journey from Portuguese Beira up to Umtali on the extreme eastern border of Rhodesia was an exciting one for Cripps. Seated in the comfort of the little railway coach, the contrast was striking between his journey and that of Bishop Knight-Bruce and his three missionary nurses only a decade before. They had first to penetrate the low malarial land; then the tse-tse fly band; and to make the long trek, climbing up some three thousand five hundred feet to the elevation of the Rhodesian highland, first with animal transport including many breakdowns, and then finally to slog out more than half of it on foot! Cripps's train reached Umtali on the evening of 6 January 1901, and he was struck with the beauty of Christmas Pass and the mountains in the region.

His first assignment was to assist a bearded Anglican priest, William Roxburgh, who had come to Rhodesia in 1898. There was a likelihood of Cripps being placed on a kind of shuttle-service between Beira and Umtali and largely involved with the British population in both places. 'I wonder what the Bishop will decide. I should much prefer (as far as I can judge) being sent off to native work, but perhaps either Roxburgh or I will have to take over the new work in Beira.' The final decision gave Cripps what he had hoped for, as the Bishop worked out a plan for him to learn Shona, the African language of the area, and he wrote: 'I think I am to stop in Umtali a while till Roxburgh goes away to a native settlement, then I am in charge for a month, then myself to go to a native settlement to learn of a native teacher' (Undated but January 1901).

The tin roofed buildings of Umtali that made up the settlement which Cripps entered in 1901 were in the typical settler style. Lions still raided the outbuildings at night and struck terror into whites and Africans alike. The rats were especially fierce. Dr Jameson reported that a particularly bold specimen had extracted his false teeth from a tumbler at his bedside and run off with them.

Arthur Cripps arrived in Rhodesia at a searching time in the life of the territory. The Boer War ground on and was not finally to be settled until 1902. While Rhodesia was not directly involved in this war, the costly struggle managed to contribute still another element to the stagnation of its fragile economy and increased the general disillusionment of Britain with the whole Rhodesian enterprise. In the beginning there had been such high hopes of Rhodesian gold discoveries that would 'surprise a dozen Rands'. The Chartered Company, after all, had secured mineral royalties which amounted to 50% of all gold taken from Rhodesian soil and it was everywhere expected that Rhodes's magic hand which had produced such fantastic profits in his diamond mine ventures in Kimberley and his famous Consolidated Gold Fields of South Africa in Johannesburg could not fail in this his greatest project of all in Rhodesia. Ten years later this nineteenth-century 'South Sea Bubble' had burst and when not a single dividend had been declared, it had begun to dawn on all but the unseeing that the twenty-one million ounces of gold that were estimated to have been taken from the ancient diggings of Rhodesia over the centuries had been laboriously screened from river beds or chipped out of modest deposits, and that while a small and continuing yield of gold might repay persistent diggers, there was nothing to promise even the faintest approach to the largest of the South African veins of gold.

Colin Leys in writing of this Rhodesian period says:

The years before 1900 were, however, wholly unprofitable. There were no spectacular gold finds, and what was found could generally only be recovered by substantial outlay on equipment and

preliminary development. European farming was equally dis-
appointing; apart from the virtually self-sufficient Dutch settlements in the south-east of the country, crop and cattle diseases,
uncertain rainfall, infertile soil and limited markets kept progress
slight (C. Lays, *European Politics in Southern Rhodesia*, Oxford
1963, p.7).

The Chartered Company's annual statements did their best to
whip up hope that fortune was just around the corner, but as one
Rhodesian mining and commercial company followed another into
liquidation, it slowly began to dawn on the investing public that
they had bought shares in a very remote dream. By 1901, £9,000,000,
just short of $45,000,000, had been poured into settling this enor-
mous territory with a few thousand white miners and ranchers, and
the railroad network, upon which the expenditure had been fabulous, did not even begin to pay its own way.

It was not the investors alone who were disillusioned. The
shortage of available African labour and the ruinous cost of supplies
in the Klondike-like atmosphere of the country produced a growing
bitterness among the white community itself. Even the missionaries discovered that they were on the most expensive field in the
world as far as living costs went and that their minute allowances
could hardly cover their barest needs. At an earlier period, when
Cecil Rhodes paid one of his lightning visits to the territory to
listen to grievances and to try to reassure the settlers, he received a
Scot who spoke for his delegation and assured Rhodes, 'I would
have you know, Mr Rhodes, that we didn't come here for posterity!'
Another when asked what he thought of the country replied,
'Well, if you want my opinion, it's a bloody fyasco!' (Lockhart
and Woodhouse, *Cecil J. Rhodes*, London 1963, p.241). Among
a large body of settlers, this temper had not changed greatly by
1901.

The pioneers themselves were a mixed lot. A third of them were
Afrikaners who had come up from South Africa in the hope of
bettering their lot, and another third were of English stock who had
lived for a time in South Africa and been deeply influenced by its
outlook. Even as a missionary, Arthur Cripps was an exception in
this respect, for like the rest of the white population, most of the
early Anglican clergy who took command in Rhodesia had already
served an apprenticeship in South Africa. This is a factor that must

be weighed in understanding Cripps's ultimate witness on the whole matter of the racial question.

There were strong, able people sprinkled among the early Rhodesian white community, such as the Lionel Cripps family and the Fairbridges whom he met in Umtali, but all too many of the white settlers helped to establish Rhodesia's name as the 'back pasture for black sheep'. The community inevitably had more than its share of 'characters'. The gold-digger 'Champagne Anderson' was one of them. He earned his name when he sold off a mining claim for £3000, cashed the cheque, treated half the town to drinks, and then ordered himself a hotel bath in champagne at something over six dollars a bottle. According to the story, the hotel-keeper heard shots in his hen-house shortly after dawn and going out to investigate, found Champagne Anderson shooting one after the other of his prize fowls, amicably explaining to him that he was sorry but that the fowls had rinderpest (a cattle disease) and had to be destroyed!

Cecil Rhodes fiercely defended his Rhodesian pioneers and his remark, 'Those who fall in the creation, fall sooner than they would have done in ordinary life, but their lives are the better and the grander' (Percy Hone, *Southern Rhodesia*, London 1909, p.170). Perhaps somewhat nearer the truth may be Percy Hone's own assessments of the character and efficiency of the Rhodesian pioneer population in which he says:

> Owing to the supply of labour being so inadequate, many men unskilled in special work or lacking in training were offered and accepted positions in which they had little or no experience.... Inefficiency, therefore, is not to be wondered at when a man who has been discharged from the Cape Mounted Police is put into a responsible position in an office, a former undergraduate of Oxford is plunged into a wholesale or retail grocer's business, a clerk from the Bank of England sets out prospecting for gold, or an unsuccessful schoolmaster determines to start farming (ibid., pp.13-14).

In his brief Umtali period, Cripps managed three trips out to St Augustine's at Penhalonga, some eleven miles from Umtali, where the Anglican Mission Centre carried out an impressive programme including an African school, an African industrial training school, and a potential Anglican theological college. Of one of these visits he wrote to his mother:

> On Tuesday the Bishop and I went out to Penhalonga.... Yesterday, we came back, he riding a donkey, I walking. I read him a good bit of 'No. 5 John St.' en route, reading the main part of the way ... The Bishop wants me, when I know some of the language, to do some Folk-Tales for publication (Candlemas Day, 1901).

> The Bishop started off for Salisbury yesterday morning: he is a rough diamond, but has some very nice points. We got on well together (Dated only, Thursday, Church House, Umtali, 1901).

Cripps remained in Umtali hardly two months, but it was long enough to know that the new country agreed with him. 'Mealie porridge is so good, also Boer tobacco. Grenadillas are rather like strawberry ice. Sunflowers, petunias, snap-dragon, and zinnias seem to do well here. I saw some pretty honey suckle the other day', he wrote to his sister Edith (Yuds).

Bishop Gaul called on him at the beginning of March to combine his African language work with serving as the missioner pro-tem at the newly-established mission station called Wreningham in the Charter region, some eleven or twelve miles distant from Enkeldoorn. Enkeldoorn itself was ninety-five long miles south-west of Salisbury. Archdeacon James Hay Upcher, who had named the Wreningham station after his old home in England, had long begged for a home furlough and now during his absence Cripps was chosen to carry on. Cripps crossed to Enkeldoorn and Archdeacon Upcher walked in to collect him for a short period of overlap at Wreningham, and then left him to embark on his first real immersion in African life at 'this populous centre of the hill people'.

Cripps wrote to his sister Edith:

> Here I am at Wreningham Mission station about ten miles from Enkeldoorn. I came out on foot with the Archdeacon on Friday. He has started off today for the town where he takes coach for Salisbury, leaving on his way to England at Easter time. You may imagine that I feel a little diffident as to the responsibilities that rest on me in looking after the native work out here. But the

Archdeacon has been kind in putting me in the way of things during our short time together (18 March 1901).

Cripps welcomed this opportunity to get to work in earnest on his Shona and for this bold adventure among the real people he had come to serve.

4

The Legend of Expendability

Oliver Cromwell once said that 'you never go so far as when you don't know where you're going'. Arthur Cripps's life, as he began what was to have been a temporary six-months' appointment to the Enkeldoorn region out of the two-year term he intended to serve in Rhodesia before resuming his life in England, was an eloquent confirmation of the soundness of Cromwell's insight. In the spring of 1901, the Bishop wrote: 'A. S. Cripps who gave up his living in Ford End to join us lost Christians is busy learning Shona and is in charge pro-tem at Wreningham and Enkeldoorn.' A year later in 1902, when Cripps's name appears again in the *Mashonaland Quarterly*, the 'pro-tem' is no longer there. Something over fifty-one years later, in August 1952, Arthur Cripps was buried in the nave of the church that he had built at Maronda Mashanu, a half-way point between Wreningham and Enkeldoorn. He had given all but some three-and-a-half years of the time between 1901 and his death to the service of this region.

Now that Cripps was stationed out among the Mashona, there could be no more putting off of the language study. The Bishop wrote that Cripps 'seems to have a real gift for languages and sees the inwardness of things with the eyes of the poet' (SPG Correspondence, 12 January 1902). A few months later he speaks of translating for Bishop Gaul and mentions casually that a friend, the Reverend John White, a fellow-missionary at the Methodist station a few hours' walk away, has offered to go over the Shona translation which Cripps and Raymond had been making of the Epistle of James. There are also comments about getting certain favourite English hymns into Shona. Nothing gives swifter evidence of the fact that you respect another people than the mastery of their language, and in this costly courtesy Cripps was as chivalrous as he was in so many other areas.

Arthur Cripps began his 'foot-slogging' by frequent turns at the twenty-four mile round-trip circuit between the African Mission Station at Wreningham and the little white settlement of Enkeldoorn. There was no proper road to travel; nothing but a small African foot-path some eighteen inches wide with almost as many twists as the trail of a snake, and there were two small 'drifts' or fords to get through in the wet season in order to reach it. Later he was to get some real jogging in weekly trips from Enkeldoorn to Umvuma, thirty-two miles away, where he took a service for the Africans in the morning and then by swift walking and jogging managed to get back to Enkeldoorn for the evening service!

> O'er the last hill I buoyant go
> With joy that mounts at every stride
> To reach my flock, my fold below—
> Hub of the merry world so wide.

This Enkeldoorn, 'Hub of the merry world so wide', was a quaint mid-Rhodesian dorp of fifty souls. There was Ferreira's place that had been turned into a *laager* in the rebellion of 1896, and there were several other trading posts, a post-office shanty, a tin-roofed hut that passed as a bar and hotel, and another set of tin sheds that housed at night the squad of African prisoners who worked on the road under armed guards during the day. On the edge of the town there was a fairly substantial Dutch Reformed church which ministered to the Afrikaners who were in the large majority among the white population of the region.

Cullen Gouldsbury, a gifted writer who came to Enkeldoorn in 1903 and who lived there for a few years, made the town of Enkeldoorn, under the pseudonym of Koodorp, the subject of a biting novel called *God's Outpost*! (London 1907). Gouldsbury described it as a village that had been 'forgotten by God and the Government' and referred to it as 'one of the might-have-beens' or as 'a gaunt spectre of blighted ambition' that had found no alluvial gold and not even been rewarded, as it had always wistfully hoped that it might, by a spur of the railroad that would have joined it to the living bloodstream of the country.

With the Chartered Company's blessing, the Dutch Reformed Church authorities had set out to establish townships wherever they found clusters of South African Dutch Reformed people and to settle branches of the Dutch Reformed Church in them. Late in 1896, while the Mashonaland Rebellion was still in progress, Cecil Rhodes met an attractive young Dutch Reformed pastor, the Reverend Albert Jacobus Liebenberg, in Salisbury. Rhodes asked him to go to the Ferreira *laager* and to select a site for a Dutch township. Early in 1897, Cecil Rhodes, at Mr Liebenberg's suggestion, bought the Vaalkop farm and presented it to the community as a site for a town. After Rhodes demurred at their wish to call it by his name, the town was given the name of Enkeldoorn (single thorn) after the name of an adjoining farm that was marked by a particularly prominent Kamuldoorn tree. Mr Liebenberg came to Enkeldoorn in the same year as the pastor of the newly-erected Dutch Reformed church and two years later, in 1899, he married. From the time of Arthur Cripps's arrival in Enkeldoorn, the Liebenbergs gave him the warmest of friendship, and he was often at their table.

Cripps was the only resident Anglican priest in the whole region and while he was charged mainly with serving the tens of thousands of Africans within the Charter District, he was also bound to minister to any of the white community who claimed membership in the Anglican Church. In the beginning this meant celebrating Holy Communion in the homes of local Anglicans and presiding at the usual family occasions of christening, marrying, burying, and visiting the sick as might be required. By 1902 when it became clear that he had come to stay, his friend, the Reverend A. J. Liebenberg, most generously offered him the use of his church for Sunday evening Anglican services. Until 1914 when the white Anglican community was strong enough to have its own church building, these evening services continued to be held, with Mrs Liebenberg playing the organ and with a good sprinkling of Dutch Reformed as well as Anglicans coming to enjoy Arthur Cripps's ministrations.

Mr Liebenberg pressed the use of his own Nachtmaal vessels on Cripps to save him bringing his own from Wreningham, and when a leading missioner came to Enkeldoorn in 1904, the two groups united for their services. General Jan Smuts when he visited Enkeldoorn was astonished to find this co-operation between a Dutch Reformed dominie and an Anglican priest and cited it as an example of what might come one day to be the way in which the English and Dutch communities might find themselves drawn closer together. These early ecumenical experiences were to grow in Cripps, and while they never dislodged his central sacramentalism, they were to carry him still further away from the ecclesiastical rigidities which were never congenial to him.

The town of Umvuma has been mentioned. It lay some thirty-two miles to the south of Enkeldoorn and it possessed a proper pharmacy and often a doctor or two in residence. Umvuma was on the Fort Victoria spur of the Bulawayo-Salisbury railway and the mail cart came to Enkeldoorn from Umvuma when the Big Sebakwe River was low enough to permit it to cross; but in the rains even the Little Sebakwe, which also had to be forded, could present a sizeable barrier.

Arthur Cripps's legend among both the Africans and the white community seems to have begun by the stories of his expendability in the service of his people, whether they were black or white, and there are various versions of his swift night journeys on foot to Umvuma for medicines when life itself depended upon them. The story of his brushing aside an askari, or guard, who was stationed there to prevent anyone crossing the dangerously flooded river, and swimming the crocodile-infested Big Sebakwe River in flood torrent to fetch medicine from the Umvuma pharmacy and return with it, is told in a variety of versions as having been made to relieve two or three different white families and as many Africans in dire need. Descendants of two specific families have told the incidents convincingly enough to wipe out any suspicion that this is mere legend, and the performance under varying circumstances probably happened more than once. Richard Nash recalls his first memory of Cripps visiting their home in Umvuma and of his being in terrible pain, as a small boy, with a tooth-ache. Cripps disappeared and in an hour or two returned with a root he had obtained from an African. This, when applied, stopped the pain in almost no time at all.

Cripps wore a broad-brimmed clergy hat, rugged khaki clothes, and enormous leather shoes that, with his incredible mileage, were always wearing out. Someone, seeing him kneeling at the altar in prayer, noticed that the soles of his boots were patched with metal from bully-beef tins. His eating habits were simple. When they were available, he enjoyed bread and eggs and tea, but he liked the African mealies, which are closely-set cobs of boiled fresh corn with rather large kernels, and he could readily manage the corn porridge (*sadza*) and the millet mush that sustained the African household.

On his long journeys he took little with him but tobacco, tea, and flour with which to make an unleavened flat bread something like an East Indian *chapatti*, which he prepared over an open fire and often lived on for days at a time. His chief indulgence was tobacco, and he was ready to fill his pipe with anything that even remotely bore that name. For long periods of time when he was on trek, he seemed oblivious of food, but when one of his parishioners offered him a meal, which they nearly all tried to do on his visits to Enkeldoorn, he would eat on and on, quite unaware of the number of helpings he had accepted. Bishop Gaul, on a visit to Enkeldoorn, once twitted Cripps about his teetotaller witness, having seen him by his own count drink six cups of tea. The Bishop told him he was jolly thankful that he, Cripps, was an abstainer from strong drink, for if he had been a drinking man, he was quite sure he would have been a roaring alcoholic!

From the very beginning of his Christian ministry to the Africans, Cripps could never deny someone who was in great want. This led to his parting again and again with his own clothing, his blankets, and his shoes, as well as impoverishing himself in the times of famine and want in order to keep the immediate African community in at least a meagre supply of grain for flour. 'Baba Cripps carried us through.' A friend gave Arthur Cripps a very fine clerical cape for his personal use, and was incensed to find that he had buried an African colleague in it. Cripps appeared in the evening Anglican service in Enkeldoorn wearing his surplice not over his cassock but over his torn khaki clothes. His friend, Mrs Diana Schultz, suspecting what had happened to the cassock, laboured with him about it after the service and discovered that, as she had thought probable, Cripps in walking to Enkeldoorn that afternoon had come across a stricken African who had no blanket and stripping off his cassock had given it to the man to put over him.

There is a story, vouched for by Canon Christelow, of Cripps conducting a funeral service for a poor African and as he came to that point in the service where the body of the deceased is tenderly laid in the open grave, he reached around to the family for the folded blanket that it was customary to place in the grave as a pillow for the head of the departed one. The family was so poor that they had no blanket to give, so Cripps quietly took off his cassock, folded it up, gave it to be used as a pillow in the grave, and went on to take the service in his shirt sleeves.

Africans have an uncanny way of coming swiftly to the point in the names that they fashion for those about them, and Cripps was given many. Two of them were Baba Mupandi—the man who went about as a poor man, and Baba Chapepa—the man who helps the sick and feeds hungry people. This man walked countless miles not only over the veld but also into the hearts of his African brothers. 'After all, our Lord walked', Cripps said once, and he always passed off lightly his long journeys on foot. 'It gives me a chance to think', 'It keeps me under the stars at night', or 'It lets me share a little of the joy of the African who is born and bred with the rustle of ten-foot grass in his ears', or 'I need the exercise so badly.' In one of his poems, 'To the Veld', he hints at what the long weariness of this endless foot-slogging had brought to him:

Nay most for all thy weariness—
The homeless void, the endless track,
Noon-thirst, and wintry night's distress—
For all tense stretchings on the rack—
That gave me my lost manhood back! (*Lyra Evangelistica*, p.72)

As it came out thirty years later in his stinging exchanges with his bishop over the missionaries' addiction to the use of motor cars, Cripps walked because the Africans walked and because he was sent as a servant to the Africans. When, as we shall see, offer after offer came to provide him with some kind of transport, he treated them all with a most cautious reluctance.

There is a medieval tale about a Franciscan preacher of great renown who was presented by an admiring patron with a swift donkey, nicely equipped with a silver-pointed bridle and a saddle, so that the preacher could cover more ground and make more sermons and save more souls. He rode it over the hills to his first appointment, tied it to the rail outside the church, and entered the pulpit. As he began to preach, the thought came to him that he may not have tied the beast securely enough and that he might get away before he could get out after the service to secure him. It occurred to him, too, that he should have brought in the silver-pointed saddle and bridle, lest someone steal them. When the service was over he hurried out and finding the donkey and his trappings intact, he untied the beast, pointed him towards his patron's village, gave him a smart slap on the flank, and said, 'Go home, I refuse to go through life tethered to an ass'.

Cripps's Franciscanism seemed singularly free of self-consciousness, but the vision of Francis to which he always felt so utterly unworthy, drew at the core of his life and without acknowledging its formative power, it would be impossible in any other way to account for the life of this strange missioner to Enkeldoorn.

There is a perverse twist to the Franciscan attitude towards all possessions which staggers those who are used to our customary morality and which often arouses sharp counter-attacks, as Arthur Cripps was to experience all through his mature life. His sister's words, 'Poor Arthur is quite mad', and his family's desperate attempt to protect him from himself summed up the feeling not only of the Enkeldoorn community but of many of his brother clergy. For in our type of society, disgrace and shame is not upon the one who has most, but upon the one who has least. But 'Franciscan shame' reversed all of this. 'The poverty of that man', said Francis of Assisi, 'brings great shame upon us.' 'It would be counted to us a theft if we should not give to him who is more needy', and Francis, giving the shivering beggar his own cloak, turns to his companion and says, 'Brother Warden, we must return what we have borrowed'.

This shocking notion of voluntarily joining the poor in their poverty and from this new vantage point of solidarity with those in greatest need, of experiencing what Vida Scudder used to call 'a communism of the heart which cannot claim in comfort what is not shared by all' has in it no blue-print for the way out of all poverty. But for Cripps it seemed to bare the nerve of the gospel ethic of our unlimited liability for all, and across a broken field of countless obstructions, inconsistencies, and stumblings, he felt its pull upon his heart, and he tried to follow it.

Arthur Cripps seldom revealed much about his own religious life and his beloved nephew, Professor Hilary Armstrong, has said how impossible it ever was to get his Uncle Arthur to talk about himself. He does mention, however, that on a visit he made to Ford End when he was up at Cambridge and Arthur Cripps was back from Africa, he observed the passion with which his uncle prostrated himself and lay prone before the altar at the early morning celebration of the Holy Communion. Time and again in

Cripps's descriptions of his trekking hundreds of miles around his vast mission parish, there are references to the morning celebration of the Mass on a convenient rock just as the sun's first rays were to be seen. He wrote to his Roman Catholic mother:

> The Holy Mass is surely the highest act of worship in all the living creation (9 July 1902).... The sun showed low behind a cloud when we were beginning our Eucharist ... After washing in a stream, we had our Eucharist. I celebrated on a rock with my head upstream towards the new sun ... The sun was but just up when ... an altar slab was found and the great service was enacted in the sunshine (*Mashonaland Quarterly,* XLIX, 1904, pp.14-17).

The One who gave all that he had and all that he was, and asks of us no less than all that we are and all that we have, seemed to Cripps to be peculiarly present upon those occasions, and like the priest and shepherd that he was, he carried around his neck on all his journeyings a small phial of the consecrated elements for sharing with the sick.

Pascal notes that in the few post-resurrection appearances of Jesus, the only place that he would let his disciples touch him was his wounds, and Cripps, if we may trust some of his finest poems, touched him in the kraals of his African friends often at the point of their most desperate need. But it is well to remember that while Francis of Assisi's intense centring upon the costly act of Jesus's death upon the cross led to the stigmata, the five wounds appearing upon his own body shortly before his death, this intensity was always mingled with his passion for the Incarnation, for the Christmas crib, and with an immense wave of tenderness for his fellow-creatures and for all creation.

Arthur Cripps, the poet, was swept with something of this same love of his Father's world and of this tenderness for all creation, and in his Rhodesian outpost he was baptized afresh with the glistening wonder of all the natural world about him. Cripps sang his own canticle to the sun on his camping trips that were almost pilgrimages to his own Alverna, the great Mount Wedza, and the endless trekking itself had elements of Francis's climbing up to his prayer caves, the Carceri, above Assisi.

He was faithful, as an Anglican priest, in closing the day with the office of Evensong. 'We had our Evensong together, then we ate much and smoked much and talked on well into the night.... Then back to our camp and Evensong and supper and prayers and singing.' There are references to his private prayers before retiring, no matter how long the journey or how late the hour of his returning. That he made frequent use of intercession in secret there can be little doubt from the legends about the power of his prayers. There are many witnesses to a certain detachment and the mingled sense of being both there and not there which are reported of him by enough sources to point towards some vein of continual recollection and infused prayer, but these were secrets hidden from public knowledge. Arthur Cripps left it to one of his Wreningham successors, Father Andrew, to write the treatises on prayer and he kept his own inner life a carefully guarded secret, except as it rings out here and there through the music of his poems. But his bishop was not blind to what was going on and he hints of it in his diocesan letter (13 January 1904), when he refers to 'All Saints', Wreningham (where dear Arthur Cripps lives and works and loves by night and by day)'.

5

The Rekindling of African
Self-confidence

Cripps's expendability in the service of his people was not the only gift that he brought to the Charter region. In many ways Cripps arrived in Rhodesia at a highly critical period for the Mashona people. Whatever may have been the character of the ancient African empire ruled over by its Monomotapa, this structure had long since crumbled away and left the Mashona people dispersed into clusters under their local chiefs. The coming northward of the splinter of the powerful Zulu tribe commonly called the Matabele had, from 1840 onwards, subjected the Mashona to periodic raids by ruthless Matabele *impis*, so fierce and so strong that the Mashona were no match for them and could only flee into the hills and the caves. In the course of these raids not only were the Mashona menfolk killed and their kraals burned, but large numbers of Mashona women and youths were taken away as slaves and cattle as booty.

Fifty years later in 1890, with the coming of the Chartered B.S.A. Company rule, the Mashona found themselves with a new set of masters who, they noted, did not in the first instance raid and slaughter. Instead they tried to harness them to dig in their mines, to work on their farms, and to build their roads and railways. Where the Matabele, with their fire and their spears, came and went away again, the whites stayed on, and there were continuous intrusions into their lives. With the new masters, too, came rinderpest and other diseases which devastated their herds of cattle; tampering with the women; expulsion from the land that housed the bones of their ancestors; and imprisonment for offences which violated no code of their own. These growing threats to the very existence of their traditional way of life aroused a great sense of uneasiness in the Mashona people.

The whites in 1896 were less than 4000 men, women, and children in the entire Rhodesian territory, and the Africans were a hundred times that many. The white Rhodesian police force at the turn of that year 1895-6 was on loan to Dr Jameson and suffered a disaster in his ill-fated raid on Johannesburg. The Matabele people in the South and West of Rhodesia had been crushed by the whites in 1893 and their great chief Lobengula_did not survive this encounter. Early in 1896, believing the time to be propitious, the Matabele made one further desperate attempt to drive out the white invaders. The Mashona to the North and East, roused by this continuous white threat to their life as a people, encouraged by the Matebele uprising, and inflamed by a group of their Mashona priests who assured them of the Spirit's command to press this attack on the whites, rebelled and in outlying places killed and burned and plundered white farms and settlements and even killed many Africans who refused to join the rebellion or who were loyal to their white employers. Both of these rebellions were decisively put down, and some 4000 Mashona were hunted out and killed, some of them by dynamiting caves into which they had fled.

In spite of the fear that sent the Charter Region farmers into laager at Ferreira's Place in 1896, the Mashona in the Enkeldoorn region had not taken an active part in the rebellion. Yet in the aftermath, they shared in the stunned, confused demoralization of the defeat of their people. Five years later, in 1901, Cripps took up his missionary labours in this kind of an atmosphere.

A wise economic philosopher, E. H. Schumacher, pondering a similar impact of one highly organized invader on an ancient Indian community and its resultant power to confuse, to paralyse, and to produce a condition of general apathy, notes that 'It was not the [military] power of the Spaniards that destroyed the Aztec empire, but the disbelief of the Aztecs in themselves (*Roots of Economic Growth*, Varanasi, India 1961, p.38). Whether he intended it or not, there is a good deal of evidence that Arthur Cripps's continued presence among the Mashona for the next half-century did a good deal to counter this tendency to disbelieve in themselves.

'I do like these people', Cripps wrote to his mother (21 May 1902) something over a year after he had come, and later he told her, 'I want to get other people to see these people as I see them, as genuine artists in their patient way' (23 November 1903). He not only liked and admired the people, but he liked and appreciated many of the elemental features of their traditional culture which in this back country were still in existence at the beginning of the century. As a poet, as a missionary champion of the Africans, and as their personal friend, Cripps expressed this appreciation not only to the white community in Rhodesia, and in Britain, but to the Mashona themselves, and it is hardly an exaggeration to say that he cared for them almost more than they cared for themselves.

As early as September 1901, Cripps wrote:

I should like to confess that my mind is eminently bucolic, a country-bred mind with a great love of ways rural, and a hearty dislike of ways urban. To such a mind, I must say, the Mashona type appeals. The Mashonas as one sees them out in the country here are pre-eminently husbandmen and neatherds. With certain allowances for racial differences, the people one meets in one's daily round might well be thought to have stepped out of the pages of Theocritus [with] ... their easy-going, happy-go-lucky life ... the women winnowing with the green spindle rift of the millet flowing about them, the boys driving out the goats by the grey rocks some cloudy morning, the men coming along the veld-track with the little black bull heavily laden. Physically one is told, the race is a poor one, but ... the Mashona race compares very favourably with the types of other coloured races one sees around here. The powers of endurance of Mashona carriers are to me, fresh from England, a revelation; and as wood-cutters, they seem to have won a great reputation among white men.

Their smithy work appears to be admirably painstaking and laborious. They gather iron stone from the hills and melt it down in an earthen furnace. Then in the pleasant arbour of a smithy, with a glowing wood fire, one plies the shaggy goatskin bellows, and another beats lustily with a heavy stone on the prospective hoe or other implement that is being shaped. Moreover the wire work with which they ornament a stick, or whip, or bottle is often a beautiful bit of handicraft. The shapes of their clay pots and root fibre baskets fill me with admiration... (MQ, xxxix, p.5).

Cripps never could say enough for the generous hospitality of the Mashona:

There is a deal of hospitable kindness. What a noble lunch I had
the other Sunday on the way into Enkeldoorn! I was pressed to
have beer but my pledge was prohibitive. Then a piece of raw
goat's flesh was thrown on the embers for me, and served in
a tin basin. No mutton chop diet was ever so very much more
pleasant or wholesome. Afterwards followed another gift, outside
of a hut, of bean porridge from a wooden ladle (ibid., p.7).

Cripps concludes this account by warning his readers, 'When you
read philanthropic and disinterested mine-owners' lamentations over
the good-for-nothing laziness of Kaffir mankind and the joyless
drudgery of Kaffir woman-kind, please be faithless and unbelieving'
(MQ, XLIX (1904), p.14). He pours out the same message in a poem
called 'A Mashona Husbandman':

> You find him listless, of but little worth
> To drudge for you, and dull to understand?
> Come watch him hoe his own rain-mellowed land:
> See how the man outbulks his body's girth!
> As new-yoked oxen ply his shoulders grand:
> He frolics, revels, ravins deep in earth:
> A kid about a swarthy mother's dugs
> He tussles greedily, and panting tugs.
> Swell in full streams, ye skies his harvest mirth!
>   (Africa: Verses, p.19)

Cripps is ready to admit that

Possibly the Mashona race does not develop those smart, well-
drilled, obsequious characteristics which have a way of finding
favour with English eyes ... I feel very hopeful that when the
nations, each in their appointed times, pour their peculiar qualities and honours into the Treasury of the City of God, the
contribution of this Mashona nation, instinct with so much spon-
taneous joy and kindness will be found to be not inconsiderable
(MQ, XXXIX, p.7).

Arthur Cripps immersed himself in this African life around him.
Almost precisely a year from the date of his original arrival in
Enkeldoorn, he gives this vivid description of his costly involve-
ment in the life of the Mashona community:

On Friday, I took such a long tramp to the Wesleyan mission and
then on to doctor a child that had been moved to a kraal some
twelve miles away ... I did not reach my destination until sun-
set ... I ate well and felt refreshed after my long trudge and
interested, as I looked around. The hut was a very well-ordered
one and looked very shapely and spacious under its dome roof.
The family gathering round the fire seemed to have stepped
out of Saxon times.... The large-limbed, soft-talking Mashona
women or girls made a very charming picture as they busied themselves over the food for the company or superintended its en-
joyment.

Then came his Evensong office and some private prayers:

I composed myself all right with a shirt and a mackintosh
pillow and my own red blanket for covering ... Just as I was
dozing off the boy of the family covered up the chickens for the
night in a basket close to me ... I did not understand exactly
the reason till I had noted the revels of the rats in the dark....

I went out to another hut to doctor a cut before settling down
to sleep. I was so tired I got some sleep to begin with, but afterwards came the consciousness of the hardness of the floor and
of those mysterious fire-attracted inhabitants of huts of whom
Raymond had warned me, 'the things that bite'. After all, they
were not so very bad, and at last came the blessed dawn (12
March 1902).

The personal cost of these occasions was not small. But his African
friends knew that he had joined them, that he was theirs, and that
for all of its discomforts, he respected them and that he respected
their way of life.

Cripps was determined to improve the lot of the people around
the mission station, and in the course of his early years there he
secured iron ploughs, brought in improved mealie seed corn,
banana, and fig trees, and even imported some bulls from England,
although he confessed that they were ultimately eaten at some
ceremonial feast. He planted a new strain of tobacco and had large
plantings of onions in the substantial mission garden. He encouraged them in their handicrafts and obtained some fine speci-
mens of iron and wire work to exhibit and sell to visitors. He
went about the building up of the Wreningham missionary station

itself and erected a school, a dormitory, and a very quaint church which, like all of Cripps's churches, made some use of the rondavel type of African hut in its design.

Cripps visited the African gaol regularly in Enkeldoorn and ministered to the prisoners there. It is one place where he reports pleasure at the shrinkage in members of his congregation! He was busy extending his reach into the vast Charter territory that was entrusted to him and beginning in friendly kraals, he ultimately built a chain of tiny centres of worship, each with a room for the visiting missioner at its side. A later missioner reported that in Cripps's territory he counted over sixty of these little out-stations which, if you went on foot, would take you well over two months of the year to get round. This missioner told someone who asked him about his housing arrangements, that he had something over sixty vicarages! These out-stations were in the course of formation in Cripps's early years at Wreningham. Many of them he could not visit oftener than once a year, but when he came, he came on foot, and it is fair to say that the God of Baba Cripps was never in a hurry. Cripps conducted their services, he baptized them, he ate their food, he sat before their fires, and the African hosts knew that in a peculiar way Cripps belonged to them. He was not blind to the shadow side of his friends: 'the fear of poisoning that makes life miserable at the kraals and tends to fix dreadful charges on innocent people', but in his religious message, he offered them a relationship that could lift them above this web of contrived accusations.

In April 1903, Arthur Cripps and his younger colleague, Edgar Lloyd, whom he was preparing for ordination, walked the ninety-odd miles from Wreningham to Salisbury in order to attend the Anglican Diocesan Synod of Mashonaland. It is the first Synod where there are records of Cripps taking an active part. Between the lines of the resolutions that Cripps proposed and the disposal of them by the majority of his Anglican clerical colleagues, there begins to be outlined, even at this early point in his Rhodesian career, what might be called *The Education of Arthur Cripps*.

While the whole Anglican body in Rhodesia was in a sense a missionary Church, there was a considerable division of labour between the few of its clergy who learned the African languages and were especially entrusted with the African outreach of the Church, and the others who found their work predominantly with white congregations. Many of the clergy, as well as the Bishop him-

self, as has been indicated, had had a period of service in South
Africa before coming to Rhodesia. Others in their continual contact
with the white Rhodesian outlook found it almost equally hard
to resist the conventional white colonial opinion about the Africans.
Cripps found these Synod experiences awakening him all afresh
both to his special task as a spokesman for the African, and to a
realization of the frailty of his powers of corporate leadership with
his fellow Anglican clergy.

At the Synod of April 1903, Arthur Cripps proposed several
corrective amendments to a set of somewhat bland 'Resolutions on
the Native Question', which stood ready for the Synod to adopt.
He suggested that they delete a section of the Resolution which
stated that 'neither individuals nor races are born with equal facilities or opportunities' as well as dropping two items, the first of
which read, 'Two things which make the native unambitious in
his work, both for himself and for others: 1st. Polygamy; 2nd. The
absence of wants', and that they also drop a further reference to
'Polygamy'.

Cripps did not condone either indolence or polygamy. He was
not prepared to accept Africans who practised polygamy as occu-
pants of the farms which he was later to acquire. But this sensitive
friend of the Africans felt inwardly that it was not the task of the
Christian Church publicly to humiliate the Mashona and his culture
but that rather it should try to strengthen them in a sense of their
own dignity and worth. The Synod records are terse on the outcome, 'Mr Cripps's amendment was put and lost', and the Resolutions as originally stated were then confirmed!

Later in the Synod, Arthur Cripps put two other concerns:
'That we desire to impress upon employers of labour alike at the
mines and at farms, of the need of rendering labour dignified and
attractive', and he went on to spell this out, 'By the provision of
comfortable and sanitary housing and feeding, proper medical
attendance, and encouragement of family settlement where local
circumstances render it advisable'. The Synod accepted the general-
ized statement but trimmed away all of the specifics. His next
proposal was entirely rejected by the Synod:

That in view of the agricultural and pastoral character of the
Mashona people, and of the fact that they have been only twelve
or thirteen years in contact with civilization, we consider that

the most desirable form of taxation to stimulate [their] industry is taxation in kind.

The second proposal that was rejected completely sounded innocent enough, but the politically-conscious clergy knew well enough that it was a direct thrust at the B.S.A. Company's proposal in this lean hunger-year of famine in 1903 to quadruple the cash hut-tax on male Africans, lifting it from 10s to £2. Cripps had approached the matter by obliquely proposing African payment of taxes in *kind* rather than in cash, because if the tax could be paid in kind, that is, in grain or goats or other products normally raised in the African reserves, it would presumably result in far less disruption in the Africans' normal pattern of life. If it had to be paid in cash, this in most cases could only be earned by male Africans being forced to leave their families behind, come out of the reserves, and work as labourers in the mines and on white farms for the extremely low wages then offered. This would mean it would take them several months of outside labour (with the sale of their precious cattle at low prices in white auctions as the only alternative) to raise the cash to pay this tax. Cripps knew all too well that this proposal to increase the hut tax was not for revenue alone, but was quite as much a thinly-veiled device for swelling the low-paid African labour available for white enterprises.

His oblique approach having failed, Cripps, in the interval since the Synod, had not only been preparing an appeal to Lord Milner, the British High Commissioner in Cape Town, but had also written, and had printed in Salisbury at his own expense, a blistering *Ode in Celebration of the Proposed Quadrupling of the Hut Tax.* He had promised his friend, Maynard Smith, that it would be 'the arraignment of the petty fathers of our petty state', and Cripps kept his promise. Back of its recriminations, Cripps had a double charge. The gross addition to the tax itself was wrong for the African who had no representation, no one to put his side of the case. And besides, Cripps was keenly aware that by the loss of his earlier lands, and by the miserably small wage that he was given when he did enter the white economy, an incalculably high 'tax' had already been levied upon the African. Then there was the second wrong in proposing to quadruple this tax in a year of famine when the African was already in desperate straits simply to keep alive.

The Ode begins with a verse:

> O wise and most paternal State
> His year of death to celebrate!
> With four-fold taxings to redress
> Your subjects' four-fold emptiness!

and concludes with the lines:

> Go glean in the fields of the harvest bare,
> From Famine meat a four-fold share!
> Apply a text as best you may—
> From him that hath not, take away!

(A. S. Cripps, *An Ode to the Hut Tax*, p. pr. 1903 1s 3d)

In the interest of haste in getting it out, Cripps left it to his Salisbury publisher to correct the proof of the small pamphlet and directed him not only to place it on sale as widely as he could in Salisbury, but to see that it got into the hands of 'the legislative assembly and the administration'. Some little time later, a copy of the *Ode* fell into the hands of his bishop, William Gaul, who felt that his young missionary-poet, Arthur Cripps, had gone too far in this matter. He at once wired asking him to withdraw the pamphlet from circulation and Cripps, out of deference to the Bishop, agreed. Writing about the *Ode* to Maynard Smith on 28 July 1903, Cripps comments with some glee, 'It had good innings I think before he wired' (U.C.).

Later bishops under whom Cripps served were either more timid or less persuasive in their handling of Cripps's pamphleteering initiatives, but even this swiftly-terminated effort was not lost on the Africans whom Cripps was seeking to defend. Once again Baba Cripps had understood them in their need and had spoken out for them, no matter what white disapproval his action had aroused.

At the same Synod in 1903, Arthur Cripps, because of his own initiative in bringing the whole matter of temperance before his Anglican brother-clergy, was appointed Diocesan Temperance Secretary, although the minute indicating his mandate was characteristically minimal: 'That this Synod considers there is room for temperance work in this country'! Cripps's interest in this matter of temperance was not simply a carry-over from his earlier British experience with vagrants, many of whom had had their lives rotted out by the excessive use of alcohol. In even his little corner of Rhodesia, he had seen among the hard-drinking whites, the brawling, the violence and murder, and bestial conduct to which a frontier country, almost floated on alcohol, could come. He also saw his Africans laid out for days after their orgies on native beer. He was no puritan and he readily confessed his own weakness in his interminable pipe-smoking, but in the unbridled use of alcohol he saw a dehumanization that he felt the Church in its witness to the dignity of man should resist.

He found that Lent was an ideal time to tackle the problem among his African brothers and having laid up his pipe for those weeks, he invited those who felt drawn to it, to give up beer for that period. He hoped that the trial of abstinence would carry over into an enduring habit. Arthur Cripps once appeared in the African church in Umvuma, robed for the service and wearing a bright red stole. He moved through the African congregation snipping off little strips of his stole with a pair of scissors and giving them out, along with an ordinary pin to any African who wished one, in order to be pinned to his garment as a reminder of his pledge to give up beer during Lent! William Penn called George Fox 'an original, no man's copy', and in his methods of temperance education, as in so many angles of his ministry, it would be hard to deny the epithet to the life-style of Arthur Cripps! William Tully, speaking of his godfather and friend, Arthur Cripps, insisted that this life-style was not eccentric; rather it was marked by a ruthless directness and simplicity.

At a meeting of clergy and laity in southern Switzerland in the reconstruction period after the Second World War, a well-known German clergyman rose to express his hearty disapproval of a project in northern Germany, where a pastor and a dozen of his laymen had dug out a foundation for a new small house of an eastern refugee family. He justified his stand by stating what he believed to be his own true vocation, 'I am called not to dig but to be a theologian'! Cripps in Africa was not so fastidious, and at this Synod he urged on his brethren the enormous value to the Africans of their clergy's own example of sharing in manual labour. He also fervently commended the practice, among the isolated and often bone-lonely missionaries, of visiting one another and he suggested in the Bishop's hearing that 'it was of great value to place priests within one day's walk [40 miles for Cripps] of each other'. He urged 'a far-flung battleline, not curtailment'. Typical of his own casualness about routine ecclesiastical duties and procedure that was to mark his whole career in Africa was the note in the Synod minute book for 1903: 'The following clergy did not present their Letters of Orders'—and Cripps's name is listed among the delinquent brethren!

With the famine behind him and a good harvest in 1905 that made him feel free to go, Cripps finally took his long-delayed furlough. He left in November 1905 and returned on 9 June 1906, just in time for his birthday. The Roman Catholic *Zambesi Mission Record* for July 1906, contains a note about the first lap of his 1905 journey back to Britain:

The Anglican clergyman of the Enkeldoorn district, the Rev. A. S. Cripps, whose mother is a Catholic and benefactress of our Mission, has lately passed through Gwelo on his way to Europe. He is a most exemplary and fervent man, austere to himself while most kind to others, and a great lover of actual poverty. To save money for his Station, he walked from Enkeldoorn to Gwelo [90 miles], he travelled third-class to Cape Town, and probably had he been asked why he travelled with so much discomfort, he would have replied, 'because there is no fourth-class'. (*ZMR*, III (1906), p.90).

Cripps returned via Cape Town and a 'collier' to Southampton. After this five-year interval in Africa, he had thought out every detail of his return to Torquay and had written ahead to his mother and sister that he would get out of the train and stretch his legs at Exeter, and be ready to greet them at Torquay. The joyous reunion after this long absence did finally take place and they carried him off to the little annexe on the property of the French teaching order of Roman Catholic nuns where his devoted Roman Catholic mother, Charlotte Cripps, and his sister, Edith, lived and there they had the Christmas weeks together.

His sister, Edith, to whom as to his mother, he wrote almost every week in those years, had worked tirelessly to handle his affairs with the publishers. She had also sent him a stream of deeply understanding and sympathetic, affectionate letters. Edith Cripps, at no small outlay of her own funds, had managed a never-ending procession of carefully chosen books and journals and papers to keep her brother in the stream of British thought in spite of his distant exile. After her death, Arthur Cripps in his dedication of *Africa: Verses* in which her name took first place, wrote the lines:

> *Edith Kate Cripps*
> I did not learn alone: she lesson'd me
> To race and battle—bearing in my heart
> The routed's anguish and the outrun's smart.

Following on the New Year, Cripps's home furlough included a fair amount of deputation work for the Society for the Propagation of the Gospel under whose auspices he worked. Cripps did not resist those deputation meetings for the SPG, for he realized that all he was able to do was carried on the shoulders of the prayers and the support of the very folk to whom he was speaking. Then, too, there was always the chance that someone might be drawn to throw in his lot for the man-hungry work of missions in Rhodesia.

Even all of this exacting deputation work, however, did not keep Cripps from visiting his brother, William, his sister, Emily Mary Armstrong, and his friends: Laurence Binyon, now an official of the British Museum; R. W. Raper, at Trinity College; Maynard Smith, a rising Anglican church historian; J. H. Adderley, and the rest. There was also time to see B. H. Blackwell and to talk of plans for the little books of poetry and the collection of stories that were soon to follow. But June 1906 did see Cripps back at Wreningham taking over his mission task from his friend, Edgar Lloyd, who had run the mission for him during these months of his first furlough.

6

Prophet and Poet

The writer and poet in Cripps showed little sign of slumbering in these early years in Rhodesia. Some months before Cripps left Ford End in November 1900, he had written to his bosom friend Maynard Smith, 'I think of getting a little book of Pastoral Poetry, or countryside songs ready for the press before I leave England, to be published in due course, if the other book [*Titania*] succeeds', and added a word of encouragement to Maynard Smith about his own writing: 'How is the 'Serpent' getting on? I do hope you won't rest until it's in print. Do stick to him' (24 September 1900). The letter also urges Smith to arrange for certain reviews of *Titania* that Cripps had promised the publisher. It leaves no doubt that the literary career and its projections is still very much in Cripps's mind even after he has committed himself to Rhodesia.

The reviews on the whole had not been unkind to *Titania*. *The Scotsman* said of it:

When it looks on Nature, it does so with a sober and stately joy. When it touches religion it does so with authority. Work like this is most akin to that of Mr Robert Bridges and readers who follow out the tradition of the pure English spirit of poetry will read the work with interest and admiration.

Another reviewer referred to it as 'a new air on an old violin'.

On board the *Hertzog* Cripps produced a sheaf of sonnets and short poems that he shared with Maynard Smith and with his sister Edith, who was to be the custodian of his literary productions. He writes regretfully to his mother and sister that he could not have 'started something big and sustained' on shipboard but pleads the motion, bustle and noise, and confinement of space as all working against this. The careful notations on his manuscript pages of Maynard Smith's criticisms and specific suggestions for correcting some of these poems show how close their friendship and concern for each other's work really was.

Cripps in Rhodesia is forever pleading with Smith, with his mother, and with Edith for longer letters to blot out his loneliness, and the evidence is strong that it was the lifeline of mail from these three and from his old tutor, Raper, which did much to keep him afloat in the first years in Rhodesia. For the rest of his life, the trek to Enkeldoorn for the post, and the return with letters, papers, and books all stuffed into a mealie sack and slung over his shoulder was a part of the weekly ritual. On the way back he added a neighbourly touch by dropping off at African kraals such mail as the post office might have on hand for any of them.

Mrs Dorothy E. Finn, who has written a much-discussed article on Arthur Cripps in *Rhodesiana* and who has made an intensive study of Cripps's poetry and its background, stresses the intense loneliness of this shy, sensitive, highly-cultured British transplant in his exile at Wreningham:

> What agonies this hopelessly impractical young Englishman endured in readjusting to close life with the African community whose language he could not speak, and in trying to cope with the day-to-day loneliness, the mind balks at visualizing (*Rhodesiana*, 1962, pp.7, 36).

While this does not tell the whole story, there is much in the first African collection of poems, *Lyra Evangelistica*, to confirm this judgement of the fierce nostalgia of one of Oxford's 'banished men' both for England and for Essex. The poem 'Essex' gives a hint of the tempting wistfulness for Ford End that could not be put down:

> I go through the fields of blue water
> On the South road of the sea.
> High to North the East-Country
> Holds her green fields to me—
> For she that I gave over,
> Gives not over me....
>
> Chelmer whose mill and willows
> Keep one red tower in sight—
> Under the Southern Cross run
> Beside the ship tonight....

England has greater counties—
Their peace to hers is small.
Low hills, rich fields, calm rivers,
In Essex seek them all,—
Essex, where I that found them
Found to lose them all. (Op. cit., pp.86-7)

And still another Essex poem closes with the line, 'Christ, is it sin to long?'

This 'zero at the bone', this gnawing ache for England which never left him to the end; this loneliness for his own kind, for those with whom he could communicate in his talking and writing with an assurance that some would respond, who would encourage him, and who would recognize him as a contributor to the inward life of his generation, was a part of the price of his Rhodesian commitment. Certainly the African world of Wreningham and the minute white world of Enkeldoorn or even of all Rhodesia offered little enough to stop this pain.

Yet Cripps knew something more than the anguish. Albert Schweitzer once confessed that when he left Strasbourg and Europe for Lambarene and Africa, he thought that he had laid his passion for theology, philosophy, and music on the altar as a lasting sacrifice, but to his boundless astonishment, as in the case of Abraham, he found that God had given them back to him with an added increment of African experience for good measure. It was a kind of confirmation of Søren Kierkegaard's notion that, at the threshold of the highest religious stage, both the aesthetic and the ethical stages in life are stripped from the one who enters this most intense stage of all. But Kierkegaard goes on to describe the miracle of how, often enough, these very stages are reconstituted and returned again, not in the wilful frame they were held before, but now available for use in the service of this new level of commitment. There is evidence that Cripps would have understood both of these examples.

Cripps, working late at night by the light of a candle in his tiny African hut and writing his daily poem with a scratchy pen and cheap ink on a scrap of paper or the back of an envelope, may seem a natural object of our avid pity and compassion. A reviewer of a book of his poems adapted, in relation to him, a line from Shelley's 'Julian and Maddalo', 'He learnt in suffering what he taught in song'. But is it not conceivable that the very isolation and loneliness of this sensitive and gifted spirit who had been plunged into the elemental starkness of Rhodesian nature and into a kingdom of bottomless human need may, through this very fact, have given him his deepest bidding to create?

Certainly there are few signs that either Africa or the missionary task muted Cripps's literary yearning, reduced his power to articulate his passion, or dried up his reservoir of experience out of which he might draw. Letters in the intimacy of the family may be too unguarded to give a measured picture of a life-objective, but six months after coming to Rhodesia, Arthur Cripps wrote his sister, Edith, in commenting upon a somewhat lukewarm review of *Titania* in the *Spectator* that had come to him, 'I mean to fight my way to power and influence in literature on the anti-materialistic side anyhow, so help me God' (5 June 1901).

Two years later in a letter to Maynard Smith, he speaks of re-reading a book that he had first read twenty years before when he was 'poetry-mad' and bound for Charterhouse School, a book which warns of how one's humanity may be reduced if the literary career becomes too professional. In the course of explaining to Maynard Smith his distinction of priest and poet, Cripps ends by contrasting priest and prophet, and half-John-the-Baptist that he was, there could be little doubt that he knew where he belonged:

I confess I think I am far more of a poet than priest at heart, a poet meaning to me something not so very different from one's priestly vows, a kind of prophet in fact. Oh the trouble I take over a sermon and a song!! I don't seem to have ecclesiastical ambitions like I do literary ones, and yet I do love pastoral work, but that seems to come in with poetry.

He concludes with, 'I am happy in my pastoral work, badly as I do it, so let it suffice for the present. If my horizon is limited, there seems to be a deal of blue in it' (30 June 1903; Godlingdon Collection, University of Rhodesia, Salisbury, Rhodesia).

Cripps's first serious literary venture after landing in Africa was a short play called *The Black Christ* which he wrote during his first weeks in Umtali. A letter to Edith in early January 1901, says:

I am trying to work the sort of idea of 'The Black Christ'; the
poetry wants polishing up: I will try and send it next week...
I don't think it is too personal: the protagonist is a Franciscan
Father. I daresay you will think it rather melodramatic (14
February 1901).

The little drama, published under his old Oxford pseudonym
with the reversed initials C.S.A. turned out to be a fierce attack
upon the whites' racial contempt for the African. It is built around
a chapel in an outpost of the Rhodesian community:

Here comes Father Anthony, the nigger's friend.... He's telling
the niggers they're as good as we are. He's ungluing society, and
yet our blighted government won't let us touch him ... It's worthwhile shutting that mouth from a business point of view.... We
must have labour for our mines if we Englishmen are to stay
here and improve the country (*The Black Christ*, Oxford 1901,
pp.9,10,14).

Father Anthony is approached, pressed, and threatened, to get
him to back a labour procurement bill and to dedicate the foundation stone of a new all-white church from which 'niggers are
barred'. He agrees to make the address but, fully aware of the
likely consequences, and after a long vigil of prayer whose course
is depicted in the play, he speaks so prophetically to the white
audience that they turn on him, stone him, and set fire to the
African Chapel. Only the crucifix with its white figure blackened
by fire is saved. 'But this, the great Rood from the shriving-place...
'tis scorched and the face is black'. To which the stricken Anthony
cries out to a fellow priest and to a white settler whom he has won
over, 'The sign! The sign of God!'
Cripps left it to Maynard Smith to find an English publisher for
The Black Christ and to see it through the press. Methuen rejected
it but Basil Blackwell at Oxford took it. There were complications
about the proofs and the first edition appeared without Cripps's
many corrections. At Cripps's own expense, Blackwell withdrew
this edition and published another corrected one. Cripps wrote to
Edith, 'I am proud of the sombre little tract of a book ... it ought
to attract notice now I think ... It seems deeply in earnest. I should
not choose it for light reading' (Rogation Tuesday 1902).

Cripps's own words, 'sombre little tract of a book', and his reference to it as possibly appearing 'melodramatic' are admirable characterizations of *The Black Christ* for it is a 'tract', almost another *Trooper Peter Halket of Mashonaland*, and it is 'melodramatic'. Having been written when he had barely touched Rhodesian soil, the query naturally arises whether it has genuinely come from the first searing encounter with the race issue in the country or whether it is an Olive Schreiner or an Adderley after-image. Most significant of all, however, is this focus on the Black Christ which is to be the central religious and social image of much that he is to write in the years to come. Maynard Smith wrote him that Marson admired the play and said he would review it in *Commonwealth*. Quinn wrote to tell him how much he liked the play which he had come upon at Oxford.

Before *The Black Christ* in its final edition was printed and launched, Cripps submitted a long poem 'Jonathan' as an entry for the 1902 Oxford University Prize Poem on a Sacred Subject and sent it to his old tutor, R. W. Raper, to turn in for him. He wrote his mother:

> I do so hope to win the prize poem with a view of getting a little money towards running up some sort of a place for teaching near the native location. There is no native work going on in the town [Enkeldoorn] at present. . . . if it wasn't a rather fine poem for a prize poem, I am strangely mistaken (23 January 1902).

In March 1902, he was still waiting for a wire from Raper, and on May Day, he had almost given up hope and speaks of being 'keen on my other irons in the fire now that this one seems to have melted away'. But by 9 July he is writing his mother, 'It was very nice to get your letter of congratulation on "Jonathan" last week: it was very warm and welcome' and he mentions a letter from Raper who said he liked the 'Marlowe' poem and estimated the Jonathan prize to amount to at least £90 ($450.00), which in the continually depleted state of Cripps's finance was a most welcome addition.

Bishop Gaul and the Rhodesian Anglican Community were proud of their Wreningham brother who had managed this Oxford prize on top of all he was carrying, and said so. Cripps could write Maynard Smith: 'The Bishop seemed very pleased with my Oxford Poem' and the Bishop wrote in his letter of 13 March 1903 to the SPG in London, 'A. S. Cripps in addition to teaching the Mashona finds time to win Oxford Poetry prizes'. But in Enkeldoorn, Cripps's winning first prize in the 1903-4 New Year's games for the one-mile walk seems to have brought him much more distinction!

During these years Cripps was sending to Edith and to Maynard Smith moving tales of fifteenth-century England which he hoped ultimately might be collected into a book.

Again, a year later, Cripps waxed enthusiastic over Charles Reade and what he did for the fifteenth-century on the continent of Europe with his novel *The Cloister and the Hearth*. Dreaming of his own calling, he wrote to Edith:

> O if I can only go on doing in a small way, what he did in a great—to glorify that splendid xvth Century. But I want to show England, not the continent. My standpoint in religion is really a bit xvth Century, I rather hope.... I somehow think our ancestors in that particular period were people of glow and vitality—or why should it thrill me so? (3 November 1903).

E. V. Lucas read the manuscript of *Magic Casements* and Duckworth of London published the book in 1905. It was placed with Michael Fairless's *Roadmender* in a well-known series of theirs. *Magic Casements* was the first of Cripps's ventures as a story-teller and it came off well. Each one of the ten fifteenth-century tales gathered in this volume is set against the backdrop of the Wars of the Roses. Yet for all of its climate of swift death, it's lightning changes of fortune, its fierce loves and hates, its deep forests and their outlaws, its wayside shrines, its anchoresses and hedge priests, its passionate faith in the Virgin and in all manner of miracles, its priests and monks subject to the rise and fall of every human frailty —through all of this, the surge of love, the curtain of hate, and the quarrelling, the being restored and healed, it is a century whose people, as Cripps depicts them, burn with an unquenchable desire to examine every facet of the well-cut diamond of life.

There is in these stories, however, more than a minstrel's skill with involvement, suspense, and a swift and surprising unravelling. There is a flavour of faith and of wonder in them. They bring an assurance of all life being in the hands of something more than man himself. They ring with a sense that this life is a swift game played for high stakes. T. S. Eliot says somewhere that we often find our true contemporaries in another century than our own. After reading these stories, it is not hard to see why Cripps felt more at home with the fifteenth-century Franciscan hedge-priest of Epping Forest than with much in what he called the 'Imperial Ecclesiasticism' of his own century.

In his letters to Charlotte Cripps, he always referred to *Magic Casements* as 'your book' and seemed to have had a deep satisfaction in dedicating this cluster of tales of pre-Reformation England to his Roman Catholic mother whom he adored, 'To my Mother C.C.M.C.'.

Cripps chose with great care the fruit of the hundreds of poems that Africa had wrung from him, and in 1909 Blackwell published his *Lyra Evangelistica* which went through three editions in England and, as a kind of African *Christian Year*, established Arthur Cripps as the missionary-poet of Southern Africa.

John Buchan, later to become Lord Tweedsmuir, tells in a prefatory note to Cripps's *Africa: Verses* in 1939 how he came to review *Lyra Evangelistica* for the *Spectator* and how this thirty-year-long friendship with Cripps began:

> In the summer of 1909 I came across a little book called *Lyra Evangelistica*, published by an Oxford bookseller. At that time I had a good deal to do with the *Spectator*, and though I did not review poetry I was moved by my admiration for Mr Cripps's work to break my rule. Soon after I had the privilege of making his acquaintance. I had been in South Africa with Lord Milner during and after the [Boer] War, and had fallen under the spell of the country, so Mr Cripps and I had other subjects of common interest besides Oxford and Literature.
>
> For thirty years I have read with a lively interest everything which Mr Cripps has written (A. S. Cripps, *Africa: Verses*, London 1939, p.vii).

John Buchan's original *Spectator* review of *Lyra Evangelistica* is headed, 'A New Poet' and it concludes with, 'This seems to us the most remarkable book of poetry issued of late'. He substantiates this high praise by speaking of Cripps as having become the poet of the Mashona people at the same time that he is their priest. He likes especially some of his short native ballads:

Full of fire and music and cut like a jewel.... In his sacred verses, there is a note which ... is absent from English poetry since Christina Rosetti—the unmistakable note of ecstasy ... He finds altars in waste places, and refreshment in thirsty lands. The slow, uphill task of the missionary is so glorified in his eyes that all romance dwells in its humblest offices ... He has always the air of a pilgrim to whom the world is a road, and he makes out of the discomforts of travel [on foot] a ritual of ease.

The Manchester Guardian of 3 September 1909, does not disclose the name of its reviewer but in its half-column review speaks of the surprise at finding under the title of *Lyra Evangelistica* 'such genuine poetry'. He notes in Cripps the frank humility of a George Herbert when he confesses his inadequacy as missioner and priest:

> Ah me!
> Flawed priest, that God should
> Choose to make of thee
> A nursery window, whence
> His babes may see
> Rapture of Saints that are, wonder
> Of Saints to be.

It praises his gift 'that suggests so much of the heat and arid spaces of South Africa and the primitive simplicity in which his people live', and concluded by suggesting that 'Mr Cripps may be a priest. He is certainly a poet'.

Noel Brettell, an outstanding living Rhodesian poet, is convinced that few poets produce in their lifetime more really great poems than you can count on the fingers of one hand. In his *Lyra Evangelistica*, published as Cripps turned forty, there are certainly some poems and some lines from poems that would have to be considered most seriously in making any such a ruthlessly contracted selection. Apart from 'A Mashona Husbandman', and 'Essex', there is his African ballad 'Love Pagan' (a cattle-price is paid for brides in Mashonaland):

> Sun-shine and hoe-shine!
> Delve and delve away!
> Hoe-head that I wrought her
> Busy shines today.

Had I but four cattle—
I would wed her now;
She is sweet of favour,
She is strong to plough

.   .   .   .

Twelve months I'll hire me
For a miner's hire—
Take the kicks and curses,
Dare the earth-damp's ire.
I will buy four cattle,
Snatch my maid and run,
She shall reap my red grain,
She shall bear my son!'
           (*Lyra Evangelistica*, Oxford 1909, pp.55-6)

Among the poems that describe the round of mission trekking through land which the African has burned over to prepare it for grazing and for tilling is Cripps's 'Ad Viam Viator':

God of the Road, I hail thee, I that hold
My roofless nights so august and so dear.
Men count their travellings trouble, toil, and fear,
But I unwilling, when my home is near,
Leave the scorch'd plains, the darkling thickets cold,—
Loth as one haled from shrine he sought to pray—
Roads are thy shrines, thou saidst 'I am the Way'.
           (ibid., p.69)

'A Counsel of Perfection' has all of the fierceness of Cripps's prophetic Franciscan passion against a missionizing that amounts to little more than the taking on of the white man's ways:

O little goatherd, would you climb to him?
From your low thatch'd hut is his vision dim?
Why have you left your tending goats and grain,
Changed your skin-belt for stuffs of gaudy stain?
So vain of temper and so close of fist?

What if you win him, little goatherd mine?
He's but a Devil dressed so tawdry fine.
Give locusts, all you caught at morning light,
Give your one blanket thin this bitter night!
Give all, strip bare and barer so to gain
The only Christ that is not won in vain!

(ibid., p.19)

In 1910 Cripps finally published the *Mashona* collection, the African version of *Magic Casements* that Bishop Gaul had so long pleaded for. The little volume of African short stories was called after a phrase of Keats: *Faerylands Forlorn*.

To read these poems and these stories that have emerged from Cripps's saturation in the life of a remote corner of Central Africa is to be convinced beyond the shadow of a doubt that Rhodesia, far from draining Cripps of his imaginative vision, has rather given it a burning-glass-like focus that can rekindle compassion and hope in the hearts of those to whom he speaks.

7

Chappatis, Tea, and Tobacco

The waters of his mission life and duties closed swiftly over Cripps as he returned from the 1905-6 furlough. He had come back just before his own thirty-seventh birthday and on that anniversary the thoughts of 'so little done, so much to do' engulfed him. A poem on 'The Shepherd' which he included three years later in his *Lyra Evangelistica* (p.40) tells of his sense of inadequacy and failure in his mission work, and yet of the fierce burning fire in his breast to begin all over again in the hope that he will fail less dismally:

> How fouled my hands! Each new-laved fleece how white!
> How lame my feet to seek them where they are—
> My sheep—among the huge rocks scattered far!
> How heavy grow mine eyes each dead of night!

.   .   .   .

> Soiled, maimed, my tale of sheep untruly kept,
> With a stern heart the reckoning I await;
> Fierce grows my love, as fierce as desperate,
> No man shall say, these last days, that I slept.

But on such a birthday there were also the small comfortings of those who welcomed him back. His African colleagues and parishioners assured him that now they lived again! An African chief 'brought me a very fine cock for a present'. There were even greetings from his ecumenical cat who had come originally from the Wesleyan mission and was known at least to have had a Methodist mother. In this matter of the cat, Arthur Cripps's great fourteenth-century patron, the anchoress, Mother Julian of Norwich, is said never to have been without the comfort of a cat in her cell, and his Zanzibar friend, Frank Weston, when not on trek, enjoyed the consolations of a magnificent cat called Simba (Lion).

Life was full. There were the Africans to be baptized in the local stream that was given the name of the 'Jordan' and when the calabash of water was poured over the head of the African seeker who was dressed in a white robe as an outward sealing of his covenant, it brought Cripps much joy. There were the sermons to be preached, upon which Cripps never reports with other than a sense of their abysmal inadequacy and something of the note of the Abbé of Cambelot. When the old Abbé was dying, he was being comforted by his chaplain and assured that if he despaired at the want of holiness in his life, at least there were his countless sermons that would plead for him in the presence of Almighty God, to which the stricken Abbé replied quietly, 'Oh my sermons, my sermons. If our Lord does not mention them first, it is not I who will begin!'

Later witnesses of a good deal of reliability such as the Reverend Richard Holderness and Leonard Mamvura remember Cripps as a simple and direct preacher whose messages were of a piece with the man who gave them, and were genuinely effective. Cripps once wrote that he was determined to avoid all 'tail-lashing in the pulpit', but one of his admirers remembers that he was fiery enough at least to make it necessary for them to put extra screws in the lectern to keep it from being torn from its moorings! But most satisfying of all for Cripps was the daily Communion service 'Life-Blood and Flesh—White Cake and Red in Cup—we break and pour thee' (*Lyra Evangelistica*, p.70). Now he was in the middle of both his years and of his chosen work. If Dag Hammarskjøld is right that 'in our era, the road to holiness, necessarily passes through the world of action', Cripps at 37 would not be excluded from these ranks by any charge of being a withdrawn recluse!

There was plenty of occasion for Cripps to renew his touch with manual labour, for at Wreningham there was the cruciform brick church to be finished before the visit of Bishop Gaul in the spring of 1907, when he was expected to dedicate it. There were also school buildings and dormitories to finish. 'I have been working at brick-making', he wrote, 'and some have been cutting grass with sickles and chopping down trees, and we are getting quite a lot of bricks and poles and long grass to build with' (*MQ*, LVIII, p.4).

At the close of the year 1906, the new All Saints', Wreningham church was finished and able to be used for a Christmas Eucharist at 3.15 a.m. and in the early months of 1907, Bishop William Gaul made his much-anticipated visit to consecrate it. In spite of his sly remarks about Cripps's 'St Sophia' or his back country 'Glaston-bury Cathedral', the Bishop was not unimpressed by its African flavour.

A month after Cripps's return from his furlough in 1906, he went to Bulawayo to attend the Second Diocesan Synod. This time he went alone, for Edgar Lloyd had left for England to have his own six months' leave immediately on Cripps's return. Edgar Lloyd was not to come back to Wreningham when his furlough was over, but was to return directly to Rusape, a point about two-thirds of the way on the hundred-and-seventy-mile south-easterly course of the Salisbury-Umtali Road. Rusape would be Lloyd's base for the rest of Cripps's lifetime and it would be from there that Lloyd would be setting out to cross the rivers and hills to meet Arthur Cripps on their famous annual camping holidays within sight of Mount Wedza. Both of them had a great passion for nature and for Rhodesia, and these treks and the week or ten days they spent together were high points in the year.

Cripps would take little with him but a blanket, a cup, and a cooking can. As provisions he managed some tea, white flour for his chapattis, perhaps a little butter or peanut butter to spread on them, and a plentiful supply of tobacco for his pipe. His two African companions that he usually honoured by inviting on this journey would carry packs and manage their own porridge materials and biltong. Their meeting place was at St Peter and St John (now St Barnabas) some sixty miles distant. There they had both a mission place of worship and a schoolhouse to sit and smoke in and to talk through the day. At sunrise and sundown there was always an occasion of worship and the Reverend Cyprian Tambo, who often made this journey in later years, used to speak of the thrill of this Mount Wedza country in almost the hushed way an ancient Jew would look at Mount Horeb or a devout Hindu would refer to the holy hill at Tiruvannamalai where Krishna himself is said to have loved to wander.

In 1933 Cripps dedicated to Edgar Lloyd his collection of poetry *All the Marvel of the Golden Skies* that was designed to become an *African Christian Year* but which was never published:

To Edgar Lloyd
Fellow Missionary in Mashonaland
Fellow Lover of the Zwinjauja
Hills and the Wedza Mountains there.

These two men had few areas of agreement and the younger Edgar Lloyd was always trying to get Arthur Cripps to be more reasonable and help him to see the other side of every issue. Edgar Lloyd, who later became a canon in the Anglican Church, and who survived his friend by a year, was much more adjusted to the world. He took a firmer hand with the African and could understand the white Rhodesians' indignation at the shortage of African labour. Edgar Lloyd resolved to marry and Arthur Cripps performed the ceremony in 1910. Twice a widower, Lloyd married a third time late in his life and, as long as Cripps could manage the journey, each of the wives, first on a donkey and then when motor cars were available, in an automobile, came along on these Wedza camping holidays. Cripps, who was well-known by the Wedza Africans, was always being visited by them. On one occasion he took a pudding that the first Mrs Lloyd had made for their dinner and gave it to his hungry African visitor; when the dinner reached the dessert stage and Mrs Lloyd could not find the pudding, Cripps, in some penitence and in much consternation confessed what he had done with it!

In spite of their sharply differing views on the Rhodesian scene, Cripps and Lloyd were each enriched by their differences and wrote each other constantly. When Cripps was in England, it was Edgar Lloyd who kept him posted on all that was happening, and even in Cripps's periods of illness and final blindness, no one was more solicitous or took more initiative to meet his friend's needs than Edgar Lloyd. He confessed in later years the penetration of Cripps's elemental intuitions about the African and how often these outwore the shrewd and plausible 'wisdom' of the temporizers and kept the eye fixed on the real issue. He himself found the example of Cripps's own Franciscan style of life impossible to follow; yet he could not readily reject the value of its witness. Among his English clerical confrères in Africa, over the years, Cripps had only two all-out friends, and Edgar Lloyd, for all of their differences of view, was one of them.

At the Diocesan Synod of 1906, Arthur Cripps's name appears

often in the discussions that were held. Perhaps most notable and characteristic of his accent was the part he took in the concern of some of the High Church clergy that the Africans should be strongly encouraged to go to confession regularly. An American Methodist bishop once told of how when he was a young minister and was being interviewed by some prominent laymen about what part his wife would take in the activities of the Church, he had replied, 'Just the same part that your wives would take'! Arthur Cripps took the same line, that confession for the African was no different from confession for the white: all may, none must, some should. The Synod minute read: 'The Rev. A. S. Cripps thought absolute freedom to use it [confession] or not should be allowed natives as with Europeans'.

By 1907, Bishop William Gaul had only carried his shepherd's crook in Mashonaland for twelve years, but the strain of the rough life there had told heavily upon him. The 1901 report in the London records file of the Society for the Propagation of the Gospel is typical. It speaks of Bishop Gaul as being again knocked out with malaria 'and taking such doses of quinine as would involve a staid London chemist in a prosecution for attempting poisoning'. He asked the diocese in mid-1907 to find his successor and this brought a flood of sorrow to Arthur Cripps, for over these six years he had come to love, esteem, and trust his bishop, William Gaul, in a fashion that was never quite to be repeated. Cripps was soon to dedicate his first volume of poems from Africa, the *Lyra Evangelistica*, to Bishop Gaul, but both upon the occasion of the Bishop's departure and afterwards in his memory, he wrote typically Crippsian tributes that swept up much that was in the hearts of the Anglican and even the wider Rhodesian community and put it in a poignant form. Cripps's gift that rose so unfailingly to mark such special moments earned for him over the years the wide acknowledgement of being Rhodesia's unnamed poet-laureate.

'Bishop William Gaul' [of Mashonaland] was one of eight poems that appeared late in the section called 'Hails and Farewells' in Cripps's *Africa: Verses*.

> As veld-fire in his time of visitation
> He would rage to and fro, and sparkling shine:
> Enthroned on mail-bags—rattling thro' the night—
> Somehow he reach'd us, soon was gone again.

No palace need we build him: Africa
Empalaced him in wattled walls of hers:
We lacked a mount for him, but Africa
On bull of hers had hors'd our Church's Prince.

His little iron-grooved cathedral-roof
And God's great veld gave back his battle-cry:
Clear from his bosom's cross his challenge flash'd,
The watchword of a hero's heart—'We can'.

Five feet of braided khaki—helmeted—
He laugh'd our Winter out, laugh'd in our Spring'.

(p.82)

Arthur Cripps took an active part in the selection of Bishop Gaul's successor. In the end, the Reverend E. M. Powell, a fellow graduate of Trinity College, Oxford, who was ten years Cripps's senior, was finally installed as bishop. He came out to Rhodesia straight from a generation of service in the poverty-stricken East-end of London and immediately from the headship of a small Anglican missionary training college for women. All in Africa was strange and wonderful for him, but for the diocese of Mashonaland the transition from the guidance of a tough, seasoned campaigner like Bishop Gaul, to this new Africa hand, immensely willing and expendable though he was, was no easy one to accomplish.

Cripps had long felt the need for women workers at Wreningham and had spoken of it at Synod. Without them the girls and women had no one to help in the intimate womanly way that is so necessary to form them in the Christian life, and to share their family problems. All of this had been so accentuated among the Mashona people by their being compelled to face the intrusions of the new white rulers of the country and their ways of organizing the productive economy of the territory which so often robbed them of their men folk for long periods at a time. Such white women could do much in the schools, and Cripps confesses frankly that many a death among his small company of Christian Africans might have been avoided if a trained woman worker's vigilant care had been given early enough.

With a new bishop taking over, Cripps had been able to carry through his long-cherished plans to add women mission workers;

to prepare the way for their coming; to build the necessary accom-
modation; and by mid-1908 to be ready to receive them. One of the
two who was secured was Agnes Saunders. She was a short, stocky,
peppery woman who often reminded the older company of those
who knew her of a miniature version of Queen Victoria, both in
visage and in her determined fashion of getting her own way. She
was the daughter of the headmaster of Cripps's old school, Charterhouse, in London, and was born in 1860; hence she was some
nine years Cripps's senior. She had come out to Africa several
years before, was already well-seasoned in living among the Africans,
and was utterly devoted to them. She poured into the work not
only herself but any personal income or gifts or funds she could
beg, and service to the Africans was literally her very life. There
were many amusing stories of her fierce identification with them.
One told of some young white mother showing Agnes Saunders
her new baby and of her responding, 'How lovely, but what a pity
it isn't black!' She managed her trips from Wreningham into
Enkeldoorn in the early days on an old sledge drawn by a horse
and as she grew older she had a kind of oblong padded box
equipped with sledge runners and painted black which brought
her to town and was known as Miss Saunders's 'coffin'.

Since Cripps, although still continuing his oversight and spiritual
service to Wreningham, had moved his own residential quarters
to Maronda Mashanu not long after the women workers settled
there, Agnes Saunders became Wreningham's very special guide.
Closely associated with Agnes Saunders in this work was Mary
Prior, a highly-educated and noble-spirited English woman who
came in 1908 and served the mission until her return to England
in 1928.

Both women had a deep respect for Arthur Cripps. His Franciscan willingness to be expendable, to work with his own hands
and body, and to keep the whole mission venture on a simple basis
drew Agnes Saunders to him, but their rhythms of working were
different enough to stir the older woman to occasional outbursts.
Cripps's holiness and his spiritual integrity made Mary Prior hold
him in the deepest reverence to the very end of her term of service,
and there is no evidence that Mary Prior and Cripps ever had other
than a relationship of complete harmony and trust.

From the beginning of Cripps's service at Wreningham, his
friends and his mother had tried to persuade him to let them

furnish him with some means of transport. A postcard in 1903 from Bishop William Gaul to H. Maynard Smith that is preserved in the archives at the University of Rhodesia reads, 'I forgot about your question re Horse. Well Cripps would only carry it when he thought it was tired and when it was fresh he'd let it run on in front. I expect he'll develop wings one day which he'll *have* to use or look foolish, so we'd better wait'. Amusingly enough, the men whom Cripps was to serve as chaplain in the command of the East African campaign had gone so far as to collect money to buy their padre a donkey for his transport when he made land sallies, but were dissuaded by an officer on the identical grounds that Father Cripps would be carrying the donkey a good part of the time!

Over the early years of his duty, however, his mother's persistent entreaties finally wore down Arthur Cripps's resistance, and late in 1906 a horse named 'Dick' seems to have been provided. Cripps wrote in his year-end letter to the *Mashonaland Quarterly* in 1906, 'Now that the priest-in-charge has, through maternal benevolence, the luxury of a horse', and later we learn that there had been much horse-sickness in the land but that 'Dick' had been spared!

Bishop Powell visited Cripps within a month of his installation and in the course of the long three-day journey back to Salisbury on Cripps's horse, 'Dick' was given a real work-out in carrying the heavy Bishop. The Bishop wrote:

Cripps will insist on my riding while he trots by my side. I don't like it. Yesterday I insisted on walking ten miles which is very good for me. But walking is not quite a treat. The kaffir path is not broad enough for my robust frame. One has to twist one leg round in front of the other and mostly the path is half cylinder which is not pleasant to the booted foot, whatever it may be to the naked one (*MQ*, LXVI, pp.3-4).

'Dick' returned from Salisbury, according to the memory of one of Cripps's parishioners, so badly marked up with saddle sores and blisters that even a long pasturing did little to restore him and Arthur Cripps, realizing that he had no business keeping an animal that he was so little prepared to care for properly, disposed of it. Cripps was himself laid up from time to time with foot infections but he seemed to be able to doctor them and to smooth out the rough places in his patched boots that caused them. He was clearly intended to specialize in 'apostle's horses' that walked on two feet.

Bishop Powell was genuinely fond of Cripps and an admirer of this Franciscan passion to live among the African poor, and of this back-veld labouring of his. But it soon became clear that the Bishop, himself, was not fitted for the continual strain of this taxing life and work. Early in 1910, after collapsing with a bout of rheumatic fever in the course of a journey to the eastern side of his diocese, he was sent back to England where he developed such serious ulcers and haemorrhages that he was compelled to ask the Rhodesian diocese for his release. He recovered eventually and resumed his work among the poor of London, and Cripps saw him regularly when he visited England on his furloughs.

8

The Middle Years
1909-1914

Cripps was soon to have his fortieth birthday. On this day in June 1909, he would be in Britain on his furlough if his plans worked out as anticipated. How did his work tally up?

> How old I grow! My labour yet is young—
> So few hours left to tend my flock so dear
> So few hours more my sickle yet may swing
> I came so late to work, and night is near.
> Hireling am I, how vain my works appear!
>
> (*The Martyr's Servant*, p.314)

But his cup ran over with the Africans' affection for him, and he hoped to be able to do more to requite it.

What, after eight years, did white Enkeldoorn make of Arthur Cripps? The Dutch people, who made up the Enkeldoorn majority, are reported to have looked upon him with a mixture of veneration and awe. He came from, and in a way he lived in, a world whose horizons far exceeded their own. They shook their heads and shrugged their shoulders and muttered often at his impractical ideas about the Mashona and how they should be treated. They were highly dubious, too, about his failure to look after himself and his own material interests with more care. But his very presence among them, as a witness to what a white Christian's life might be like who was prepared to live with Africans in the midst of their poverty, was highly unsettling.

Cripps knew well enough that he was not really a part of this poverty any more than Francis of Assisi was in his day, for his own life style was freely chosen and he could always withdraw. But now as he moved up towards a decade of it, putting his life

and his salary and his personal income and all that he could beg
from his friends into it, he knew that he was beginning to play
for keeps.

There was a variety of reasons why Cripps felt that he should
return to England for a brief furlough in 1909. His mother was
ageing and had not been well; his widowed elder brother, William,
was to be married again and wanted Arthur to perform the ceremony; it became increasingly clear to him that he should secure
some land on which his African friends could live and where he
could build up a mission station after his own heart, and this
required money which he hoped to find help with in England.
Finally there were always useful conferences to be held with publishers, for not only was *Lyra Evangelistica* just making its début
in England, but he had both a boys' book, *Two of Them Together*,
and his *Faerylands Forlorn* to offer, and three or four more projected books of stories to discuss. In his straitened finances, these
books, if they came off, might help with the purchase of the farms
that he felt the Africans needed so desperately.

The Diocesan records for 25 March 1909, contain the minute:

> The Bishop read a letter from Rev. A. S. Cripps asking for a
> grant for passage 3rd class to England on a furlough. It was
> resolved on the proposal of Mr Lotts that the treasurer be
> authorized after communicating with Mr Cripps to book a 2nd
> class rail and passenger steamer passage for Mr Cripps.

The unsettling presence of Arthur Cripps had made itself felt not
only at Enkeldoorn but even on his brother clergy! For a third-
class boat passage was steerage and not conducive to the rest and
recuperation that an Anglican clergyman on furlough might have
reason to expect! The *Journal* of John Woolman, an American
Quaker whose life was much given over to removing the institution
of human slavery, tells of his concern to visit England in 1771 and
to witness among the Quakers there to the evils of the English
involvement in the slave traffic that was being pressed between
Africa and the American colonies. Woolman was drawn to take a
steerage passage on a ship for London, believing this to be in
keeping with his labour for the oppressed. The incident in the
Journal closed with the lines, 'Friends having expressed their desire
that I might have a more convenient place than steerage, did not

urge it, but appeared to leave me to the Lord'. (Whittier edn, N.Y. 1871, p.248)

Arthur Cripps replied to the Diocesan Finance Board on 14 April 1909, thanking them for:

Their generous decision as to my boat fare and salary ... As to my railway fare [the journey from Gwelo to Cape Town and return], believe me I am not merely prejudiced but acting on principle in refusing your kind offer of a second class fare. I could undertake to use the money you offer me for a 3rd class (8-berth cabin) in the 'Walmer Castle' leaving Cape Town on May 19.... Please book the class and cabin I have asked for. (Letters in Diocesan Strong Room in Salisbury, Rhodesia).

He indicates incidentally that he had travelled quite acceptably by the same class on his previous furlough in 1906. Apparently the diocesan authorities 'did not urge it' further, but also appeared to 'leave [him] to the Lord'.

With Wreningham in the hands of Agnes Saunders and Mary Prior for these furlough months, Arthur Cripps made the fortnight-crossing to England in ample time to share his fortieth birthday with his family. A fellow passenger in steerage was in such desperate need of a decent suit of clothing that Cripps had given him the one he had been wearing and, to his mother's consternation, he arrived at Stoodley Knowle in Torquay not only carrying, as always, his mealie sack and a biscuit tin tied up with a cord, but on this occasion he wore simply his mackintosh on top of his trousers and shirt! 'Arthur is quite mad' was the household word, but they loved him and managed to replace the clothing. He had brought along a fair supply of his home-grown Wreningham to-bacco and the perpetual smudge from his pipe led his mother to inquire if there was any chance that by mistake they had cured the Wreningham cabbages instead of the tobacco!

On 7 June 1909, some three days before Cripps's fortieth birth-day, he officiated at William Cripps's marriage to his second wife, Janet Bungard Colston, at the parish church in Chigwell. His brother's first wife, Fanny, had died in 1904 and Janet Colston had helped to nurse her in her last illness. Elizabeth Cripps, a great favourite of her Uncle Arthur's, and the twins, Christine and Janet Cripps, were born to Janet Colston Cripps.

Cripps's need for money to buy a farm must have been much in his talk with his mother on this visit, and there is evidence that she did provide some funds with which he was able to cover a substantial part of the purchase payments on the larger of two farms, Muckleneuk, which he went about acquiring on his return. No proper papers seem to have survived about the precise details of the acquiring of these farms. The first 'Muckleneuk' was apparently over 3000 acres and while it was thin granite soil and land was cheap, Cripps must have made a sizeable down payment out of his mother's funds. As for the balance, a change of owners left him in mid-1910 with a £200 debt to the Amalgamated Properties of Rhodesia and he had to borrow £160 of this from the diocesan treasury.

There is a note of some desperation in the letter he writes to the Archdeacon in which he mentions how many Africans have already moved on to the farms. He did not stop with the Muckleneuk farm, however, but also acquired a 'small' farm of 1700 acres, called Money Putt, with some time to pay off its cost. On 27 July 1911, he asked the diocese for a further grant of a loan. In return for this loan he promised to erect his own buildings useful for mission purposes on the farms and not to involve the diocese in their cost even though the diocese will benefit from their existence as a further base for Anglican missionary labours.

Douglas Aylen, a Natural Resources Board official whom Cripps knew at the end of his life, speaks of *three* farms having been acquired. But only the two are mentioned by Cripps himself when he wrote in the *Mashonaland Quarterly* in a letter dated 27 June 1912:

> We call the whole tract of country Maronda Mashanu (The Five Wounds). It is made up partly of a farm called Muckleneuk which has over 3000 acres in it ... Muckleneuk is paid for. The other part I am allowed to use on a permit of occupation and hope to pay for it in time. It adds perhaps 1700 acres to the other farm so that altogether there is quite a large estate for us to work over, with ever so many people living on it for us to try to help along....

The acquisition of this land was the realization of Cripps's dream. Now the Africans whom he permitted to settle there could herd their cattle and goats and cultivate their gardens and their

bees in peace. He, too, was now free to arrange matters as he saw
fit on his own land and could build a mission church and develop
a station after his heart's desire. But few gardens of Eden do not
sooner or later disclose their serpents, and Cripps's Maronda Mashanu region was to be no exception. From the very outset he was
burdened with debt for the land itself to say nothing of the
buildings, the fencing, the educational instruction, and the bottomless needs of his tenants. Always he hoped vainly that his writing
would supplement his small private income and his maintenance
as a missionary, and might lift this burden from him.

The anxious note in the letters about the placing of the manuscripts was not alone to comfort the author's yearning to be wanted,
and to be listened to, but in a very blunt way to help pay off the
growing blanket of debt that seemed always to threaten him. As
he was known to be generous to a fault, Cripps's family looked on
his obligations as a bottomless pit and chose to send any gifts to
him through neighbours like Diana Schultz, who had a standing
contract with his family to see that Arthur Cripps got two khaki
suits a year and boots as needed.

The *Lyra Evangelistica* that had appeared in 1909 went through
three editions in Britain in the next two years and greatly heartened
him, but like all of his books, it brought little in the way of
substantial royalties. Mowbrays of Oxford published a boys' book,
Two of Them Together, in 1910, which was reprinted in 1911 and
1913, B. H. Blackwell of Oxford published two volumes of Cripps's
stories about Rhodesian life: *The Brooding Earth* and *Bay Tree
Country*. Both had about them a little of *The Black Christ* flavour
of plumbing the white Rhodesians' conduct with his African
brothers and finding it pitifully wanting. Now, however, after a
decade of living in the country, these stories are seasoned with
rich, robust, first-hand observations. They portray a lover's quarrel
throughout, for Arthur Cripps loved Rhodesia with a love so fierce
that he could not abide its baseness. Flashes of self-disclosure blaze
out as the stories unfold.

Cripps's poems continued to appear with B. H. Blackwell issuing
Pilgrimage of Grace: Verses on a Mission in 1912 and also *Pilgrim's
Joy* in 1916, when Cripps was already a chaplain in the East
African Campaign. Duckworth of London published, as a part of
their well known Road-mender Series, both *The Martyr's Servant*
(1915) and *The Martyr's Heir* (1916) as Cripps's contributions to

the spiritual history of Central Africa. In them he tells in the most moving way of the witness and martyrdom of the early Portuguese missionary of the Society of Jesus, Don Goncalo de Silveira, at the hands of the African Monomotapa in 1560. It is impressive that Cripps in these middle years of his life managed such an output, writing his books often by candlelight in his single-roomed rondavel at Maronda Mashanu with a full day of mission activity and visiting already tucked behind him. At the peak of his literary activity in September 1912, when he required and received still further loans from the diocese with which to build his new mission church at Maronda Mashanu, the following note appears in the Diocesan records: 'Resolved that Rev. A. S. Cripps be thanked for his generous offer of the royalties from his books but that the Board cannot see the way to accept same.' He had tried to pledge to them all that remained of his treasures as an earnest of his gratitude for their willingness to give him these loans to help him over his immediate need.

Meanwhile late in 1910, Bishop E. H. Powell had been replaced by Bishop Frederick H. Beaven. Bishop Beaven was then 56 years old, a graduate of Durham University in Britain, and a former dean of the cathedral church in Salisbury. He was very much the white European layman's choice for Bishop and knew little of the missionary work of the diocese. There was in the early years of Bishop Beaven's episcopate a relationship of friendly respect between Arthur Cripps and his Bishop. The Bishop visited Enkeldoorn and Wreningham in May 1911, and Cripps interpreted his words into Shona for the Africans.

Cripps attended the Diocesan Synod of 1912 presided over by Bishop Beaven. He proposed the inclusion of African delegates at the Diocesan Synod, these African delegates to be chosen by the congregations of different races, and suggested also that the Bishop 'be asked to invite personally native congregations to send qualified representatives of their own race to the next Synod' (Diocesan Synod Minutes, 15 September 1912). Cripps's motion was 'indefinitely deferred', although it is interesting to note that its substance was presented nine years later in 1921 by Archdeacon Etheridge and was promptly enacted. Cripps was always too early, and was known to be too committed to the one side! He had a second rejection at the 1912 Synod, which he might have predicted, when he objected to the calling of one of the chapels of the new cathedral in Salisbury after Cecil Rhodes, who had died a decade before. He suggested that prayers for him as the State's founder in the course of the Commemoration of Souls was quite enough!

Much of Cripps's heart at this time was poured into the building of the new mission church of the Five Wounds on his Muckleneuk farm. Cripps had always refused to believe that a way could not be found of incorporating the Africans' own building styles into the fashioning of a Christian church building, where the African as he worshipped would feel both at home and uplifted. Now he was free to carry out his dream as far as the poles and the piled stone and the mud and the thatch would permit itself to be shaped.

One of the still unravelled riddles of Rhodesia is precisely who is responsible for the original construction of the fantastically piled stone walls, stone pillars, and ornaments of the ruined Zimbabwe which stands in solitary vigil some twenty miles to the south of Fort Victoria. Did the Africans themselves build it and, like the Benin people of Nigeria, establish once and for all the stature of their artistic skills? Or is it a work of Egyptian or Phoenician or Arab architects and craftsmen? Feelings ran high according to which side you favoured in this controversy.

Cripps was convinced that Zimbabwe was of African origin, and he seems to have been as much haunted by Zimbabwe as by Francis of Assisi and the stigmata when he fashioned the Maronda Mashanu church with its five pillars of stones, its rondavel thatched roofs, its rugged altar with a clay floor studded with pebbles, and an almost Hindu freedom for the birds to share in its worship as they wheeled in and out and were looked upon not as intruders but as our sisters the birds. Built in 1912 out of poles, stones, mud, and grass for thatch, it could hardly be of repair-proof durability. No African expected this of even his best hut. The Reverend Richard Holderness, who visited it in its later, renovated form, remembered that 'It was full of holiness and mystery and reminded me of Zimbabwe ruins'.

When the Archdeacon dedicated it in 1913 and when Bishop Beaven came later to celebrate the Eucharist at its altar, both complained of the protruding pebbles and of the dust on their shoes, but Cripps's only reply was that it was a penitential altar and that they usually served it in bare feet!

Cripps's single-roomed hut of adobe and thatch which, like the Maronda Mashanu church, was renewed on his return from England in 1930, stood only a few yards from the church, and it was here, apart from a few short intervals and three and a half years in England from 1926-30, that Cripps was to spend the remaining forty years of his life. Just at the back of the Maronda Mashanu church, there is a holy hill which Cripps used as his 'Carceri', climbing up often for prayer and meditation.

Catherine Charlotte Cripps, his devoted mother, died at The Knowle in Torquay in 1913 and Cripps dedicated *The Martyr's Servant* to her. Deeply respecting her son's Franciscan passion, she nevertheless wanted, out of her small estate, to provide at least a bare subsistence for him, come what would, and she knew that in order to do this she must tie up the principle in an un-get-at-able trust and make sure that he had only the disposal of the small annual income which was to be made over to him in quarterly payments. It is presumed that the trust may have had in it some £6000 which, at a conservative 3%, in those days would have yielded some £180 ($900.00) a year. William Cripps, Arthur's elder brother, as a trustee, saw to it that his mother's intention was carried out even in the face of Arthur's impetuous demands to draw on the capital itself for spending on the urgent needs of his African brethren.

In the summer of 1914, the diocesan records show Cripps's salary being paid to another, presumably to take his place while he went for a short and urgent furlough to England to see his sister Edith at Torquay and to arrange his own affairs for the future. He prepared a will during this time and the dates of 11 September 1914, attached to his own signature and to that of his Torquay witnesses on the will, indicate that he did not return to Rhodesia until mid-September 1914, after the fateful outbreak of World War 1. In this will, he left his British royalties and his British funds to his sister Edith, setting up a separate group of executors to deal with his farms and property in Africa. The executors in Africa consisted, significantly enough, of his intimate Anglican clergyman friend, Edgar Lloyd; John Hallward, an Anglican monk of the Community of the Resurrection working in Eastern Rhodesia as a missionary, to whom he was deeply attached; and Mary Prior, his most trusted woman co-worker at Wreningham. They were to serve only as long as they were resident in Rhodesia and his property was to be devoted to 'Purposes of evangelization and education of natives'. If it is true that we may know what we treasure most by what our minds most readily turn to when given a liberty such as that conferred when making a last will and testament, it is clear that for Arthur Cripps, at this strange and revealing moment, apart from his responsible concern for his unmarried sister, Edith, it is his African brethren who are his overwhelming passion.

9

A Million Acres

When Cripps returned to Rhodesia in the autumn of 1914, he found almost every able-bodied man trying to discover how he could be spared in order to offer himself in some service of the war. In this the clergy were no exception. Early in 1915, Cripps volunteered to serve for a year as a chaplain and was sent to Lake Victoria in the East Africa Campaign. His decision to enlist came after an agonizing inward search. There was his mission work in Charter District that needed every ounce of his strength to hold it together. There was his growing conviction as a Franciscan Christian that war itself was in defiance of the way of Christ. There was a strong feeling that involving and spending the blood of tens of thousands of innocent and disinherited Africans in the white man's struggle was wrong to the core. Yet he loved Britain and the values of its culture when it lived up to them. He also had a strange confidence that as a chaplain he might be able in some small way in addition to his religious duties to serve as a shield and as a spokesman for the rights and the interests of the African labour corps.

Cripps lengthened the year by agreeing to serve for an additional six months, refusing to take any pay for this latter service. Well before that period was up, the immediate objectives in German East Africa were reached and the Lake Command was disbanded, which permitted his return to Enkeldoorn. His book of poems *Lake and War* that Blackwell published in 1917, tells the story of his deep disillusionment and of the stinging confirmation of all his grounds for hesitation in joining the war.

In the course of his military service, the patriotic Bishop Beaven had offered Cripps an honorary canonry which Cripps politely declined. Whether it came from Cripps or from some wag, the word got round that Cripps had said of the *honorary* canonry, 'Why have a stall without a manger?' But the grounds of his refusal were far more obvious.

After this soul-shredding period as a chaplain in the East African Campaign, Arthur Cripps found a great healing in the old rhythm of his daily life at Maronda Mashanu. But before this first year (1916-17) of Cripps's restoration to his mission round was over, word reached him that the Imperial Commission on the Native Reserves of Southern Rhodesia, which had been set up in the early months of 1914, had completed its report on the finalization of the boundaries of the Native Reserves of Southern Rhodesia. He learned, to his alarm and dismay, that instead of recommending that a vast increase of cultivable land be taken from the enormous pool of the B.S.A. Company's as yet unassigned ('unalienated') land and set aside to augment the present inadequate reserves for the use of the rapidly growing African rural community, the Commission was actually proposing to reduce the existing total acreage of the native reserves by over a million acres.

Cripps also learned that in this year of 1917, in the heat of the terrible World War 1, where Britain was being drained of her blood and her treasure avowedly in order to preserve human rights, the High Commissioner in South Africa and the Colonial Office in London had received and had accepted this Imperial Commission's report, and that only an Order in Council remained to complete its implementation. Cripps always felt that the pivotal issue for the Mashona was access to more land. His own farms were evidence enough of his resolve not to wait for the State to act but to take the nettle in his own hands as he made his own small packet of land available to his local African friends. The reserves and later the African Purchase Areas were not the only solution to the land problem, but for Cripps they were 'our best makeshift harbour of refuge' and later on he called them a 'windscreen tempering the blustering overseas breeze to the shorn black lamb' (*The African Protectorates*, 1935, p.105).

The 1917 announcement of the Reserve Commission's report had a history behind it that still needs to be unravelled fully. Cripps and his few Rhodesian and British colleagues were themselves to make history in the next decade in the way in which they exposed the land-for-Africans-question to the British public, to the Privy Council, to the British Parliament, to the Colonial Office, and ultimately to the 'Responsible Government' authorities of the Rhodesian territory when these men took over from the B.S.A. Company administration in 1923.

The Southern Rhodesian Missionary Conference had pressed for an enlargement of the African reserves as early as 1908 and had been briskly turned down, with the B.S.A. Company's chief surveyor, Atherstone, insisting that he would like to see a million acres chopped off the existing African reserves! The S.R.M.C. raised the issue again in 1913 and suggested that nothing short of an impartial Imperial Commission could make an adequate assessment and finalization of the 'badly delimited and insufficient African reserves'. Within a year such an Imperial Commission had been appointed. The original mandate suggested including in its number someone from the Native Affairs Department who knew African needs and African opinion, but this was not done.

The British authorities both in 1894 and in 1898 had ordered the B.S.A. Company to set up adequate reserves for the Matabele and Mashona people and to include in them 'a fair and equitable proportion of springs and permanent water'. They had insisted that all B.S.A. decisions on land questions were subject to review by the British High Commissioner in Cape Town. By 1913 well over 50% of the Africans resident in Southern Rhodesia lived in these reserves.

From the very beginning, the resident missionaries were highly critical of the land that had been assigned to the Native Reserves. Professor Per Hassing of the Boston University School of Theology in his excellent unpublished doctoral dissertation on *Christian Missions and British Expansion—Southern Rhodesia*, notes (p.239) that missionaries complained about the 1894 land assignments to the Matabele as being of poor quality land, wanting in water, malarial, and containing too much bush. He also speaks (p.241) of the 1898-1902 reserve assignments as made by B.S.A. men who were ignorant of the number they were providing for; that they themselves did not know the land well; that the boundaries were badly marked. Now, however, the Imperial Commission in 1917 had given its final, and for the African, its grim decision and it had been promptly accepted by the Colonial Office.

Cripps knew well enough the forces he was opposing. In spite of the steady transition of authority in Rhodesia during these years from the B.S.A. Company to 'Responsible Self Government', the white economy under whatever banner, hated the reserves. It wanted African manpower for its mines, its farms, and its factories and it resented African reserves of land where the African might make his own livelihood and, with some modest improvements, pursue his earlier way of life in relative self-sufficiency. But Cripps's faith in the British trusteeship principle, which for him meant that Britain's ultimate and primary responsibility lay in seeing that the rights of the native population of her territories were vigilantly safeguarded, was at stake in this issue of the African reserves.

In 1915, John Harris, the Secretary of the venerable Anti-Slavery and Aborigines Protection Society in Britain, visited Southern Rhodesia to look for himself into the land question. John Harris did not meet Arthur Cripps on this trip to Rhodesia, but he heard enough about his championship of the African to be drawn to write to him when Cripps returned from the war. A good deal that we know about this next chapter in Arthur Cripps's life is to be found in this A.P.S. correspondence which, ironically enough, is now owned by and housed in the archives of Rhodes House in Oxford.

The local farmers and authorities in Enkeldoorn had long ago learned to respect and even to fear Cripps's readiness to appear in court cases and to speak up with his impressive presence and voice for an accused African or to press for justice when a native police officer or a farm employer had exceeded his authority and mal-treated a black man. Cripps was also known in government circles in Salisbury not only for his poetry, but also for the treks on foot that he made from Enkeldoorn in order to report some injustice to the African which he believed needed to be brought to their attention. It was not unheard of in that well-stratified but chivalrous British society of the day that this poet-priest, who had walked a hundred miles to cause them trouble, might even be invited to spend the night at the British Resident Commissioner's house. After all, he was a Trinity College man and a man of letters and a priest of the Church of England—even if he had 'gone native' in a curious sort of way and could be counted on for an opinion biased in the Africans' favour!

But until now Arthur Cripps's championship of the African, apart from his books and his poetry, had nearly all taken place inside the minor league of Southern Rhodesia itself. Now, however, Cripps was to make his appeal to a more powerful team and to lay his case before the home representatives of the Colonial Office itself. To go over the heads of the Government officials of the territory and to use British public media like *The Times* and the *Manchester*

Guardian and the *Contemporary* and printed pamphlets that might have a wide circulation in Britain, or to collaborate with British missionary or philanthropic groups who, through friendly M.P.s, might be able to ask awkward questions on the floor of the House of Commons, was highly embarrassing to the local Rhodesian authorities and was sharply resented by them as a mild species of treason. There is however, a good deal of evidence to indicate that the very capacity to get this kind of hearing of the Africans' case among the vast British middle-class whose public conscience on issues of colonial injustice, if such issues could be established, was able to make itself sharply felt in the British parliament—was a political leverage of no small significance, and one that the Rhodesian officials, although they despised it, were shrewd enough not to underestimate.

John Harris wrote to Arthur Cripps from the Aborigines Protection Society in London on 19 September 1917:

I am delighted to see that you are back in Rhodesia. This will help us enormously because the struggle is becoming keener.

I send herewith in advance a set of proofs of the questions and answers in the House with regard to the cutting down of Reserves. At present the Rhodesian Reform Committee (a group of fourteen able public figures, six of whom are M.P.s, with the Rt Hon. J. W. Wilson, M.P., a member of the Privy Council, as their Chairman) is pursuing exactly the policy you recommend, namely to get a postponement of the Government action until after the Privy Council Judgment (on the ultimate ownership of the unassigned land in Southern Rhodesia). We have some reason to think that we are going to succeed but you can be quite sure of this that we shall leave no stone unturned to defeat this iniquitous proposal.

(This and the following letters, in Chapters 9-12 unless otherwise designated, are quoted from the A.P.S. Document Mss. British Empire, S.22, G.159-69, to be found in Rhodes House.)

Arthur Cripps had received a note from the Education Department in Salisbury dated 20 July 1917, stating that two sites in the Sabi Native Reserves about which Cripps had apparently inquired, are on land 'which has reverted to the British South African Company'. This was fair warning that, although no Order in Coun-

cil had as yet implemented the Imperial Commission's recommendations, the B.S.A. Company was blandly assuming that this additional million acres had already 'reverted' to them and had passed
on this word to their staff! Cripps sent the letter along to Harris
for the arsenal of parliamentary questions from the floor of the
House, and Harris asked for any further evidences that 'the B.S.A.
Company is taking action upon the question of the Reserves' prior to
imperial sanction being officially given to this Commission report.

The B.S.A. Company in the person of its famous Chairman,
Dr Starr Jameson, had managed by his premature gloating at the
1917 annual meeting of the Company, to provide both Cripps and
Harris and the Rhodesian Reform Commission with still more
alarming confirmation that the B.S.A. Company already took this
cut in the reserves as a *fait accompli*. Dr Starr Jameson's words
to the B.S.A. stockholders in the 1917 report of the meeting were:

> Now, gentlemen, besides the record of progress, in various direc-
> tions, measures have been taken to clear up ambiguities and
> uncertainties, to consolidate our position, and so make our prop-
> erty more valuable. Our native areas have always been in rather
> a fluid state. A Commission was appointed by the Imperial
> Government to inquire into the necessary areas to be set aside
> for natives ... The needs of the natives, both now and in the
> future—after careful examination by this Commission—which
> travelled all over the country, accompanied by the surveyor
> general—have been amply provided for, and the net result is
> that more than 1,000,000 acres of land have been added to the
> land which may be leased for white settlement. That means
> really that you people get another million acres odd of what
> is called unalienated [unassigned] land in the country. That is
> very satisfactory...

The correspondence between Cripps and Harris during the following months is most revealing of the extended dimension of Cripps's
role in putting the Africans' side of the case in this matter of the
Native Reserves in such a way that all Britain might hear it. Harris
wrote Cripps on 18 October 1917:

> Many thanks for your kind letter. In my view of this wicked
> proposal to cut down the reserves, we are about to ask the Secret-

ary of State to receive a deputation. I will let you know the results. The facts that you gave us are most valuable.

'The facts' had come very especially from a pamphlet, *A Million Acres,* giving both the vital statistics regarding 'this Chartered Company windfall and the natives discomfiture'—a pamphlet written by Cripps which he had apparently hoped Harris might get published for him in Britain. Early in 1918, Cripps forwarded to Harris a letter from the Reverend John White, his Methodist missionary colleague, who was to become his most intimate friend. John White was a skilful missionary statesman who had not only risked his own life for the Mashona in the 1896-7 Mashona Rebellion, but had continued to be a tough champion of African interests in Southern Rhodesia. Rueing the fact that of all the Christian missionaries, only Etheridge and Cripps had actively testified before this Imperial Commission, White tellingly explains how innocently and almost contemptuously the missionaries had tended to look upon this wartime exercise of these 'Imperial' commissioners—all of whom at one time or another had worked for the B.S.A. Company and who were therefore compromised from the outset by the conflict-of-interest issue.

John White's letter of 13 March 1918 which Cripps sent on to Harris, read:

When this Commission was investigating I was asked to give evidence and refused. I thought that the composition of it was so palpably one-sided that the [British] Government would take no notice of its findings. Had things been normal, I am sure they would not have done so. This war has meant the passing of many things that would have been more fully investigated and probably turned down. The fact that such a large number of Natives in the whole of this country are living on private farms and paying in many cases big rents, proves conclusively that the land set apart for them is either unsuitable or very insufficient ... It seems to me a shameful thing that when quite a number of people [Africans] are assisting the Empire in this gigantic struggle against tyranny that this time should be selected to rob them of their heritage.
                    With kindest regards,
                      Yours Affectionately,
                        John White

Arthur Cripps did not hesitate to go ahead with his own pamphlet, *A Million Acres*, and to publish it privately in Salisbury with a generous supply mailed overseas for John Harris and his other British friends to distribute there. He sent a copy of *A Million Acres* to Sir Drummond Chaplin, the B.S.A. Company's Resident Administrator in Salisbury, and promptly received a spirited reply from his private secretary:

I am directed by the Administrator to acknowledge receipt of your pamphlet entitled 'A Million Acres'. His Honour regrets that your zeal for the natives should lead you to make such an undeserved and offensive attack upon those responsible for the administration of this territory ... the unfairness of your action seems to His Honour to be quite inexcusable (Correspondence to and from Sir Drummond Chaplin, 1918-23, in Central Africa (National) Archives, Salisbury, cited by C. A. Ranger, *State and Church in Southern Rhodesia*, Historical Assn. of Rhodesia and Nyasaland, Local series 4-6).

In November 1918, Cripps assured Chaplin of his hope to 'do what I can to represent my honest views in the matter at home [in Britain]'. Chaplin referring to Cripps in some later correspondence notes, 'He certainly is a very difficult person to deal with' (ibid., p.7). From the point of view of the Chartered Company and its authorities, this must have been an understatement!

In the next two years from 1918-20, Cripps not only helped John Harris with facts and figures, with arguments, and with scrupulously careful corrections of A.P.S. approaches on this issue of the wrong of the general shrinkage of African reserves. He also narrowed his focus and concentrated on a special area of that shrinkage in the Sabi Native Reserve that was in his own Charter District. He had originally testified to the Commission insisting that they must not disturb the Native Sabi Reserves. But a portion of the Imperial Commission report dealt with a proposal to take a twelve-mile strip running through the very heart of the best land in the Sabi Reserve, together with certain other excisions from this important African Reserve, some 291,800 acres in all, on the ground that a railway was being projected to run through the territory some day that would require six miles on each side of it for white settlement. It threw in for good measure the argument that the Africans did not need this territory anyway!

Cripps as early as 21 February 1918, prepared a closely-worded memorandum on the subject of this Sabi Native Reserve issue to present to the British Resident Commissioner in Salisbury. In it he marshalled his case for some initiative on the part of the Resident Commissioner to prevent the finalizing of this impending wrong. This first brief statement contains the accusation of bias and of conflict of interest in that the Chief Surveyor, Atherstone, who served on the Imperial Commission as an alternate for F. J. Newton, had publicly stated in August, 1908, and again in 1911, that he favoured a million-acre reduction in the Native Reserves! It also notes the small acreage of good, bad, and indifferent land per head of the African population which these Reserve recommendations allow. Two days later, on 23 February 1918, Cripps sent a copy of this statement to Harris with a note asking if it could not be used in shaping a question to be put in the House of Commons. 'Please observe and move for questions or a question about it or its subject-matter possibly, should you think it worthwhile. God-speed!! A. S. C.'

The reply which Cripps received on 30 October 1918 from the British Resident Commissioner's secretary brushed off his protest and closed with the line:

I think you will be well advised to accept without further protest the Commission's decision and you will find, I feel certain, that in the result of putting the decision into effect, the natives will suffer no hardship.

Cripps sent this reply on to Harris as a 'provincial document'.

Cripps continued for the next two years to work on the scandalous inequity of taking this twelve-mile strip of some of the best land that remained to the Africans of this Sabi District, and he found a staunch colleague in his friend, J. W. Posselt, the Native Commissioner for the Charter District, who advised him and joined in the protest which finally led to a dropping of that project.

Once again in preparing this pamphlet, Cripps was not content simply to give a routine memorandum on the Sabi Reserve Affair, knowing that if British opinion was to be roused, it must also have something more personal in it. So a few weeks before his return to Britain late in 1919, on his long overdue furlough, Arthur Cripps walked the length of the Sabi Reserve and in his sketch, *The Sabi*

Reserve: A Pondered Protest, which B. H. Blackwell of Oxford printed early in 1920, and which was widely spread about in England, he gave among other things a vivid day-by-day account of his walking through the territory which was at stake. In an appendix, he included a first-class account of a similar journey made two years before by a friend for whose integrity he could vouch, also a very impressive fifteen-page appeal *To the Crown*, a memorandum on Natives and Lands addressed to the British High Commissioner in Cape Town which Cripps prepared and had privately printed in August 1919.

Two other events are notable for Arthur Cripps in 1918. B. H. Blackwell of Oxford published still another book. This one was called *Cinderella of the South*. He gave it a subtitle, '*South African Tales*'.

The tales were more of the lively, whimsical sketches of Rhodesian whites of all species facing their testing, in the crucible of that sun-drenched land, with the black man and their treatment of him as a kind of plumb line against which they were being measured. The earlier volumes of stories, *The Brooding Earth* and *Bay Tree Country,* had begun this series, but in his continuation, there is perhaps more self-revelation than in either of the earlier volumes.

A young seventeen-year-old African named Cyprian Tambo, who had come to Umvuma for work and not found it to his liking, stopped at Maronda Mashanu and asked Cripps if he could stay on with him there. Cripps was clear that he could not at this point father and support another, and discouraged him. But Tambo did not leave, and Cripps, after some testing of his tenacity, relented and by the time a year was out, he saw in Tambo a young man of real promise as a teacher and perhaps as an Anglican priest. He had meant to send him to the Anglican school at Penhalonga for five years of schooling, but a quarantine there at that moment led him to entrust this highly promising youth, who was to become almost a disciple of his, to John White of Methodist Waddilove with the jocular but no less deep-felt caution that he was not to become a Methodist! At a very critical moment in Cripps's own life, a dozen years later, Cyprian Tambo was to remind Cripps of this parting warning that he had received from him at his leave-taking for school in 1919.

From the summer of 1919 to Cripps's autumn sailing for Southampton aboard the *Llanstephan Castle*, plans were being made for this furlough that the war and its aftermath had postponed for so long. Once again Agnes Saunders and Mary Prior would be in charge at the mission. This time Cripps felt he had a special job to do in Britain. 'I hope to sail for England, Nov. 7th., if it may be and to try to do something for the Native Land Case there' (2 October 1919).

10

Fiery-hearted Men Must
Speak Out

During his 1919-20 furlough period in Britain, Cripps made his headquarters with his sister, Edith, at Torquay, but with all that he had to do in helping to mount the case against this shrinkage of the Rhodesian African reserves, he saw less of her than he had done on previous visits. The decision of the Privy Council on the actual ownership of the unalienated land (including the reserves) had already been made public. The Crown assumed the ownership of the land—not as the custodian of the Africans, as the A.P.S. had tried to establish, but in its own right. Harris wrote to Cripps on 29 July 1919, that the B.S.A. Company has

> lost its claim not only to the Commercial but to any ownership of the land; its local concessions were declared valueless ... As far , as the natives are concerned, the one substantial gain is that the Company's claim to the ownership of their reserve has entirely failed. It is now the duty of the A.P.S. to approach the Secretary of State,

the Crown now holding title to the land. This was presently undertaken.

Lord Milner, when they called, while understanding and most friendly, gave them little satisfaction, so that they had only the last recourse of a visit to the Prime Minister, David Lloyd George, and to attempts through the personal intervention of the Archbishop of Canterbury and the initiating of a deluge of diocesan and Free Church appeals, to impress the Prime Minister with what was at stake in this Native Reserve affair.

Soon after his arrival in England, Cripps had gone to London to call on Bishop Charles Gore, who urged him to see the Arch-

bishop of Canterbury. Harris had prepared the matter most carefully with letters to the Reverend G. K. A. Bell (later to become
the great ecumenical Bishop of Chichester) at Lambeth Palace
and the exchange of letters between them is revealing of their
impression of Arthur Cripps. John Harris wrote to G. K. A. Bell
on 5 December 1918:

> My immediate object is that of informing you that the Rev.
> Shearly Cripps has just arrived from Rhodesia. It is happily a
> fact that whatever native oppression has occurred in one section
> or another of the Christian community has thrown up a defender
> of the oppressed who has seen more deeply and felt more keenly
> than others, the suffering of the unfortunate natives ... In
> Rhodesia this imperishable honour has fallen to the Anglican
> Church through Shearly Cripps ... Shearly Cripps has cared
> nothing for social ostracism, ridicule, and censure ... with a
> single eye to the loyal adherence to the Christian faith, he has
> made himself not merely the defender of the natives, but their
> wise counsellor and friend. In short those of us who have been
> privileged to go through the fire with him, owe him a debt we can
> never repay.

Cripps was invited to spend the night at Lambeth Palace just
after the turn of the New Year (1920), but the only detail of the
visit that is still extant seems to be a tale, either true or apocryphal,
of Cripps, with his biscuit tin under his arm, arriving for the
night at the front door of Lambeth Palace immediately after
having fallen into an open coal hole, and while quite undamaged
in body, hardly looking even his Crippsian best. The attendant was
horrified and in high dudgeon sent him round to the back entrance and slammed the front door in his face.
In February, Cripps drafted a long letter to the Archbishop
summarizing the situation and the urgent need for a correction
of some of these glaring inequities before the Order in Council
should be issued to finalize the Imperial Native Reserve Commission's recommendations. There is a record of a question put by
one of the members of Parliament to Colonel Amery in 1920,
querying whether attention was being given to this Commission
proposal to take the twelve-mile strip in 'the area referred to by
Rev. Arthur Shearly Cripps in his brochure, *The Sabi Reserve*'.

Colonel Amery replied that the matter 'was under consideration as it seemed to be excessive and further it was delaying the Order in Council finally proclaimed and delimiting the Reserves for all time' (p.26, Southern Rhodesia Missionary Conference Report, 1920). It was apparently being made increasingly clear to the Colonial Office that the land question for natives in far-off Rhodesia was becoming a public concern in Britain!

There is a discerning letter written to Arthur Cripps by John White on 13 February 1920, that shows their closeness:

In going home [to Britain] just now, I am quite sure you have done the very opportune and courageous thing. Unless someone can fight the cause as you are doing, the case will go by default ... If you think there is anything I might help you in, you won't fail I hope to commandeer me ... I noticed questions were asked in the House once or twice and suspected that you were the inspiration thereof.

The first four months of 1920 were full ones for Cripps. Harris conferred with him continually and opened the way for an interview with Major Wood, the future Lord Halifax. It was Harris who saw to it that Cripps was included in an interview with Colonel Amery at the Colonial Office and had arranged that on 19 February 1920 a question in the Commons was asked of the Under-Secretary of State as to 'whether he will give assurance that these papers [a White Book] will be complete and will include a letter of explanation addressed to the Colonial Office by the Rev. A. S. Cripps of Mashonaland?' Harris supplied Cripps with important names to whom he might send letters and copies of *The Sabi Reserve*, which had just appeared. He might then be able to follow up these letters with personal interviews. Copies of the pamphlet were widely circulated in the House of Lords and to some forty others who might be concerned. There were articles in the *Church Times* and in the *Contemporary Review*.

With his furlough at an end and having done what he could in Britain for the African cause, Cripps sailed for Cape Town on the *Suscon* on 14 May 1920, for his return to Rhodesia. He had not been in Rhodesia long when he got word of Bishop Beaven's having published a letter in the London *Times* for 11 June 1920, paying high tribute to the fine race relations existing within Southern

Rhodesia and the great kindness with which the natives were treated by the whites and challenging any who might give another impression. The Bishop's public letter contained no hint of a reference to the native reserve lands which was the vital subject at stake. John Harris replied in *The Times* of 14 June 1920, with a telling letter summing up the land issue. Harris wrote Cripps on 17 June 1920. 'This is a "felon blow" by the Bishop of Southern Rhodesia [*sic*]. Alas that it should be written in future years that amongst those who forsook the natives...'

Cripps replied on 14 July 1920:

Many thanks for sending me the Bishop's letter. I suppose he means well and is in his own way conscientious. Personally, I quite sympathize as to the picture your vivid words conjure up of the disciples of the Black Christ forsaking him and fleeing. There is some stern work in front of us (*D.V.*) assuredly. Well God bless your Society!!!
    Yours ever,
    A. S. Cripps.

There is a third P.S. to this letter in which all charity for the Bishop recedes and Cripps explodes as he cites a report from the *West Sussex Gazette* of another speech of Bishop Beaven's:

The Bishop emphatically denies that there was oppression of the native races, who, he declared, 'were dealt with in that spirit of even-handed justice for which the flag of Britain stands'. [Cripps adds,] 'God forgive him if he really said that. Would it possibly help the Native Cause if I challenged him to disown or withdraw this statement. or if he would do neither, to take three months notice from me?

John Harris replied to this explosion on 10 August 1920, 'On the whole it is better to leave the Bishop alone.... Some day he will see his mistake. Let us reserve our energy for better ends than denouncing one who should be our colleague'.

At the close of this memorable year, 1920, Cripps wrote to John Harris on 1 January 1921, and quoted some prophetic lines about the ultimate African reaction which the *Bulawayo Chronicle* had deleted from a letter of John White's:

This unawakened race does not perceive yet the injury that has been done it. But one day it will arouse itself, become articulate ... and then ...? But this is for the next act in this sombre drama.

It is uncanny to find Arthur Cripps's devoted friend, Frank Weston, bishop of Zanzibar, driven later in the same year to an almost identical despair by his struggle to keep the labour-hungry white colonists in Kenya from persuading the British Government to permit them in 1920 to continue the precedent of the forced labour laws for Africans which had been imposed in the depths of the East African War. Later on Maynard Smith wrote to Cripps about Frank Weston's part in the struggle:

He loved Africa and like you he loved the Africans. It is three years since it was largely through him that the forced labour-regulations were abandoned. He stormed Milner in the fastnesses of the Colonial Office; he roped in an unlikely team like the Archbishop [of Canterbury], Lord Haldane, and Dr Oldham and drove them into action (Roberts Coll. Undated but late in 1924).

Bishop Weston nearly lost his case through the yielding of the local Anglican bishops of Uganda and Mombasa, but through a widespread revulsion on the part of the Anglican clergy and bishops in Britain and of the missionary establishments of many other denominations, and assisted by J. H. Oldham's tireless diplomacy, these men withdrew their consent, and the aroused conscience of Britain insisted that nothing must interfere with the protection of the rights and the steady advancement of the African population in this colony.

In the depth of his gloom, Bishop Frank Weston, too, wondered if he should not step aside from the whole Establishment. At just such a moment, he wrote to Cripps from London:

My inner mind is to cut myself off from the British and throw in my lot entirely with the Bantu—I can at least bear my own witness ... of course it would mean resigning my See. Hitherto I have thought it possible to help my flock because I had a

See. But if one cannot save them from serfdom by one's position, one may as well suffer with them as an individual.

This comment was incorporated in a biography of Weston published six years later by Cripps's old friend, Maynard Smith. Anticipating criticism for including such frank statements, Smith said, 'I am glad when I think of Frank's generous indignation ... Hot-headed and fiery-hearted men must speak out if wrongs are to be understood: more temperate men are also needed if wrongs are to be righted' (Ibid., Introduction). In both Weston's and Cripps's case, they stayed where they were. Frank Weston saw this forced-labour matter in Kenya through to its withdrawal, and for the next five years, at least, Cripps did not change his station.

The Southern Rhodesian Missionary Conference held its first post-war meeting in Salisbury from 16-19 June 1920. The Conference was high-lighted by an unusually sharp attack on the Aborigines Protection Society and on Cripps and Harris for their work in Britain on the Native Reserves. This attack was made by Archdeacon Etheridge who knew well the inequities for the African that were contained in the Reserve Commission's recommendations, for he had himself pressed for such changes as an increase of the Umtasi South Reserve and had actually proposed a review of those situations where the Native Commissioners' recommendations had been rejected by the Commission, and also suggested a plan for setting up Native Purchase Areas.

When the Archdeacon had finished putting his case, John White, Cripps's staunch Methodist colleague, spoke briefly and then had to leave the meeting. Cripps was left alone to refute in detail each of the Archdeacon's allegations and to deplore this ungracious and ungrateful attack upon the very instrument, the A.P.S., which had in its efforts in Britain almost singlehandedly held back the Order in Council for these three years, thereby making possible the very review of these cases of conflicting evidence which the Archdeacon was proposing.

In spite of Cripps's spirited defence, the meeting by a large majority adopted Etheridge's resolution. At a Government House tea party for the missionaries (from which Cripps was absent) some of the missionaries, according to a dispatch of Sir Drummond Chaplin, the B.S.A. Administrator, told him 'that they wished the resolution had been even stronger' (T. D. Ranger, ibid., p.7).

Later when Archdeacon Etheridge found that the *Commonwealth*
article, which he cited principally in his attacks, had falsely put
Harris's and the A.P.S.'s position, he apologized in a letter to the
press. But the mischief had been done; for the local Rhodesian
press had printed his speech in detail and had commented warmly
on receiving such support from so prominent a clergyman.

Harris, on 6 August 1920, wrote to Etheridge:

The blow you have dealt the cause of the natives is a heavy one—
though of course unintentionally so, because, from experience,
we know too well the use that will be made of your speech—a
use against which 'explanation' will be of little avail.

On the matter of setting up special Native Purchase Areas,
Cripps, who had already proposed such a need in spite of the
Africans' theoretical right to purchase land anywhere, pressed the
matter vigorously and was pleased to find the Chief Native Commissioner, Herbert T. Taylor, on his side. Professor Per Hassing
(op. cit., p.250) notes that 'Cripps, supported by White, sent a
lengthy opus to the Colonial Office urging upon them the necessity
of such a provision (Native Purchase Areas)'. (Cripps to Colonial
Office, CAA,N/3/19/9). The (London) *Times* for 9 March 1920;
12 March 1921; and for both 28 March and 26 October 1922, as
well as an article in the journal *East-West* (pp.211-26) all carried
Cripps's concern on Native Purchase Areas to the British public.

When on 12 November 1920, the Order in Council implementing
the Imperial Native Reserve Commission's recommendation
finally appeared there was, to be sure, no restoration of the million
plus acres which Cripps and Harris and John White had struggled
for. But the results were not lacking in consequences. Most important of all, they had, by their vigilant action, delayed the Order in
Council for three years; had made possible an extended debate,
and had permitted the people of Britain to become acquainted with
the issue involved in the Africans' need of land in Southern
Rhodesia. While the Sabi Reserve shrinkage was not officially
altered, the railway and the twelve-mile strip proposal was quietly
abandoned, and although Cripps and White in 1922 and 1923 kept
pressing the A.P.S. to get this abandonment made 'official', in
point of fact, it simply faded out. There were serious adjustments
made in the reserve strips in the north-east bordering the Portu-

guese territory and in several other regions, as the result of the lively debate which had been stimulated. Finally, it should be noted that enough sentiment on the land issue for Africans had been roused to open the way in the decade that followed for the adoption of a vast, if ultimately questionable, Native Purchase Area programme.

John White, on 2 August 1920, closed a letter to Harris, 'I often hear from Cripps. He is a great and fearless fighter. Nothing will turn him aside from what he considers the path of duty'. A few months later, on 6 December 1920, he concludes another letter to Harris, 'Cripps has gone into an area that is in quarantine because of smallpox and may be there for a month or so. If you do not hear from him, you will know the cause'.

11

Medical and Legal Missionaries

The turn of the new year of 1921 marked the twentieth anniversary of Cripps's arrival in Beira to take up his 'two-year' tour of duty with the SPG. There was a special celebration in March 1921 to mark Cripps's twenty years of service to Charter District, and black and white friends both showed their gratitude for his faithful service.

Some ten years later, Arthur Cripps in a letter to his brother, William, dated 14 January 1932, wrote:

People talk about the need of medical missionaries, but in a country like S. Africa, what a call for legal missionaries there is. If I had my time over again, and were going to these parts of Africa (South or East) where the African is up against it, I think I would try to qualify in law (R.C.).

In these years, it is hard to see how even full legal training could have equipped him for any more adequate service in defence of the Africans and their rights than he had in fact succeeded in rendering.

What no professional training could ever have given Cripps, and what more than anything else marked his twenty years of service as a Christian missionary to the Mashona people was his unabashed Franciscan-like identification with them and with their lives. It was not a theoretical or an exclusively inward identification but an identification with their poverty, their simple style of housing, of food, of sleeping on the floor, of sanitation, of getting from one place to another on foot. It was in being at one with them in their leisurely and chivalrous courtesies in meeting and greeting and conferring. Though he was English to the core, it would still have to be confessed that in these twenty years he had in a very real sense become one with them. When, after 1921, Cripps attended the Anglican Synod at all, he slept with the African clergy and often ate with them, even though in the beginning he was the only white clergyman to do it.

Some years after this, one of Britain's apostles to India, C. F. Andrews, wrote a biography of John White, Cripps's closest friend. This little volume contains a chapter about Cripps himself which came largely from a memorandum which John White had supplied. John White's assessment of this costly personal identification of Cripps with the Mashona people is revealing:

When the annals of Rhodesia are faithfully recorded, and the personalities who have influenced the country most potently and beneficially are written, the Rev. Arthur Shearly Cripps will occupy a very high place. At present no one appreciates the true value of the service that he is rendering. Colonists look upon him as a strange and eccentric man, whose teaching and treatment of the natives is doing a great deal to spoil them. For his character, they have a high regard, but think nothing of his judgement in matters of this kind ... Cripps is a champion for better treatment and kinder relations between the races. He lives almost as they [the Mashona] live on the very simplest food and in a hut similar to those the Africans themselves occupy. And so he comes near to those people and they can see in him a true representative of the Christ who dwelt on the earth amongst us. If he hears of a Mashona sick twenty miles away, he will take his blanket on his shoulder and march to see him, sometimes doing the journey in a single day. He is always urging upon the government to give more medical help to the needy African people.

For twenty years this man has honoured and blessed me by his friendship. Its value has not been merely sentimental, though I love him as a man. But he has set before me a high ideal. His frequent letters have reminded me of tasks to face and urged me to toil on. Few of us who know him can walk in his steps; we tread falteringly in the way that he blazed. He is our modern Francis of Assisi—in many respects a worthy successor of that great saint ... This is the man who has influenced me more than any other man in Rhodesia (C. F. Andrews, *John White of Mashonaland*, London 1935, pp.120-1).

There has been a good deal of debate on how far the missionary may rightly go in identifying himself with those whom he means to serve. The case for 'moderation' is well known. A recent writer on missions from the Roman Catholic communion would defend the 'irregular' Cripps utterly in his immoderate type of identification:

> The missioner is not supposed to be detached. He is supposed to love his people, to become one with them. The great missioners of our day have not been cosmopolitan. Charles de Foucauld in his hut at Tamanrasset, Vincent Lebbe, leading his army of stretcher bearers over the hills of Shansi, were not just holy priests who realized that all men are brothers. They were missioners to particular peoples who loved so fiercely, and who defended them and their customs from attack ... Christ came not as a man of no nationality but as a Jew. The missioner must establish the Church in *this* area among *this* people. (J. A. McCoy, *Advice from the Field*, Baltimore 1962, p.52).

The Reverend Cyprian Tambo was once asked to tell something about the kind of religious instruction which Arthur Cripps gave him. His reply was that it was not any instruction but rather 'the way Cripps lived' that drew him and his friends into the Christian way. 'He handed me books but he didn't teach much. It was from his life that we learned.' This life was a life that was linked to their own.

The backdrop to the Rhodesian drama against which Cripps's life and work unfolded was being constantly changed in the early years of the 1920s. The British government, with the help of the Lord Cave Commission and some subsequent groups of assessors, finally made a settlement with the B.S.A. Company for the large deficit which it had run in administering the colony, and withdrew them from their governing role. This cleared the way for the new Constitution and for the Rhodesian plebiscite which rejected the proposal for Rhodesia to join up with South Africa. The new Constitution for Southern Rhodesia's 'Responsible Self-Government' did not go quite as far as to confer Dominion status upon the territory. All legislation dealing with Africans' affairs was still to be subject to an Imperial veto. In turning the territory over to the elected settler white leaders of the country, there was also included in the Constitution, in a notable 'Article 43' an earlier provision that Africans possessed the right, together with all others, to purchase land anywhere in the country. This was done in spite of the strongest white Rhodesian protests.

Neither Cripps nor John White was sanguine about the future of the African under the 'Responsible Self-Government' which began in 1923. Both know well enough that this word 'Responsible' when spelled out in this situation meant no more and no less than that 40,000 whites and twenty times that many, or 800,000 blacks, were to be governed by a white settler legislature that was responsible only to the 40,000 whites who had elected them—and 'human nature and party politics being what they are, the rulers look after their own interests first'.

In the period between 1921 and 1923, Cripps had prepared an impressive memorandum on *Native Rights Under a New Government* that expounded this conflict-of-interest principle. Cripps and White were not content only to urge the retention of the Imperial Veto and 'Article 43' in the Constitution. They used this fluid period to raise in Britain a consciousness of the need for making absolute the titles to the Native Reserves so that they would not be nibbled away for roads, railways, or government installations. They also used it very especially to ventilate the terms of the so-called 'non-racial' franchise in Rhodesia where income and property qualifications were such as to keep all but 60 of the 800,000 Africans from being encouraged to qualify for this franchise. They proposed, too, some stopgap measures such as the establishment of a network of Native Councils, and a plan for getting at least the beginnings of African representation in the Southern Rhodesian Parliament even though it might have to be through elected or appointed European representatives of African interests. With John Harris and the A.P.S.'s services at their disposal, this process of ventilation was assisted, as before, by well-framed questions to the Colonial Secretary which were put from the floor of the House of Commons by willing members of Parliament such as Captain Wedgwood Benn, Henry Cavendish Bentick, and P. Wilson Raffan, and by occasional parliamentary delegations to the Colonial Secretary to press the matter further.

John White expressed his pessimism at the situation in a letter to Harris, 9 October 1923. 'The new [S.R.] Government is not of a kind that will brook a moment's disfavour to gain a reform for the Natives.' But Cripps did not think that his hope for a movement for establishing large Native Land Purchase Areas that already had considerable backing from the Chief Native Commissioner and the 'splendid new Governor, J. R. Chancellor', whom Britain had appointed would make it necessary for the Government to 'brook disfavour' in order to set these up. It was to this project that Cripps determined to devote himself for the next years even though occasional diversions to fend off undesirable legislative proposals that affected the Africans might temporarily take him from it. John White had long ago agreed that these Native Purchase Areas were essential and had written Harris, 6 December 1920:

> They [the Africans] have the legal right I know to buy land, but practically they are unable to become owners of land. A white man would hardly sell to a native. If therefore the government set aside adequate areas for such purchase, it would be a good step forward. It would not take away their legal right to become purchasers elsewhere if they found land available.

Cripps and White had been sharply overruled on the land issue in the 1920 Southern Rhodesian Missionary Conference assemblies, but when the 1922 and 1924 meetings were held, it was another story. The first resolution in 1922 asked for 'portions of unalienated land adjacent to the reserves to be offered for sale to natives who desire to become individual owners of land'. White moved the resolution and the records of the 1922 session note that 'the Rev Arthur Cripps seconded the resolution in a fervent address'. The motion was unanimously passed.

John White wrote to Harris, 6 November 1923:

> As far as the land purchase scheme goes, my friend Cripps is not a bit too emphatic when he says the alternatives are, 'Now or Never' ... so you will keep that in mind. All sane, humane men here say it should be done. Nobody raises a finger so far to do it.

In 1924 at the meeting of the S.R.M.C., Arthur Cripps gave a paper on *Land Purchase*. The situation had now moved along, and the Government had indicated that it would move to set up a commission to go into the Native Land Purchase Areas issue. But now the question had been raised of whether, if it did set up facilities for Native Land Purchase, Article 43 of the Constitution might be dropped and the Africans exchange this Constitutional right to buy land *anywhere* for the new facilities which would be offered them in literally segregated areas where only Africans might live.

The real matter at issue, however, was not only this matter of segregation but was that of who was to have access to the vast pool of as yet unalienated land. Cripps, who saw the issue very clearly, had no intention of giving up this African claim to buy land any-where which was embodied in Article 43 of the Constitution, unless the African in return got a proper share of this unalienated land. Cripps's resolution that followed the paper is quoted in the 1924 S.R.M.C. *Proceedings*:

> That while this Conference welcomes the Government's intention to face the question of the provision of native purchase areas, it puts on record its expression of opinion that clause 43 of our Constitution ought not to be surrendered except on the terms of a fair partition of the unalienated land.

The Government in 1925 went ahead with the appointment of the Carter Commission to examine the whole issue of the unalienated land and to make recommendations for its dis-position.

Cripps was as vigilant as ever that the new Carter Commission should stay within its terms of reference and confine itself to Purchase Areas *outside* the Reserves. When word came back to him that the Commission had taken evidence about the African Reserves, implying that some of those precious reserves acres might be utilized for African Land Purchase, Cripps immediately took the matter up with Sir John Chancellor, the British Governor of Rhodesia.

The Governor discussed Cripps's accusations both with the Premier and the Attorney General and found that Cripps's inter-pretation of the Commission's terms of reference was correct. The Governor wrote to Cripps on 8 May 1925, that 'The question of Natives being permitted to purchase and own portions of the

reserves does not fall within the terms of reference of the Land
Commission, and the Government do not desire the Commission
to report upon it'. Soon afterwards Cripps had a warm letter from
the Assistant Chief Native Commissioner, H. M. Jackson, written
on 26 May 1925, asking after Cripps's health because he had not
been able to meet the Governor:

> However we hope you are fit again. The Governor told me to tell
> you that he had written you ... and hoped that you had gotten
> the letter. You know, don't you, that you scored a distinct vic-
> tory over this Commission business. I had no idea that things had
> gotten so near the edge. You were right, I was not. You achieved
> a service and we look to you in recognition. Best regards.

On 15 August 1925, Cripps wrote Harris of the incident and
added:

> Our Governor seemed to quite gratefully approve of my protest
> when I saw him Sunday, 15 July. He seemed to think that
> the usefulness of the Commission might have been spoilt if the
> idea of a Purchase Policy within the Reserves had been handed
> on.

Cripps wrote to Harris on 26 September 1925, that 'I gave evidence before the three members of the Lands Commission on 23
September.' In his evidence Cripps had pointed out that 31,000,000
acres of alienated (assigned) land was already in the hands of the
small white community of 40,000 persons as against the now (1925)
almost 900,000 Africans being in possession of little beyond the
21,000,000 acres in the African Reserves. When, therefore, it came
to the dividing up of the remaining 43,000,000 acres of yet unassigned land, it would be only fair that at least one-half of this
43,000,000 acres be assigned to Native Land Purchase Areas, if the
Natives were to be asked to give up the Article 43 in the Constitution. If, however, the Commission was not prepared to pin
down the future so specifically, Cripps suggested a second alternative. They might leave Article 43 as it stood and settle for
10,000,000 acres (the difference between the present white 31,000,000
acres) to be taken from the unassigned land total at once and designated for Native Purchase.

The expected report of the Carter Commission did not actually appear until well into 1926 and it very definitely did not take the form that Cripps had suggested in his 'evidence'! Rather the Commission recommended the allotting to whites of 17,500,000 acres immediately for settlement and speculation, out of the 43,000,000 acres of land as yet unassigned, and the setting aside of 8,000,000 acres for African Purchase Areas. They further recommended that in the light of making available 8,000,000 acres of the unassigned land to the Africans, Article 43 should be struck from the Constitution! The remaining 17,500,000 acres were to be left for 'future consideration' but with no guarantees that the Africans would get any share of them. In 1930, after four years of discussion, this recommendation became the law.

Arthur Cripps prepared a manuscript of book size, *Africa for Africans*, that covered the whole land issue. When it appeared in 1927, with a highly commendatory Introduction by Sir Philip Kerr (later to become the Marquess of Lothian), its plea for a fairer distribution of the land to Africans of Rhodesia was widely set forth in the reviews of the book and in the discussion that followed. The matter of the Commission's report and the action to be taken was discussed for the next three years and the S.R.M.C. did its share of it.

It is interesting to see the way the Missionary Conference, with John White on its Executive from 1920-30, and serving as its President for two terms in 1926 and 1928, had seemed to become a body of considerable weight in the affairs of the new Rhodesia. The Government's concern to attend its meetings and even to submit matters like the Native Preachers Bill to the Conference for its advice, as it did in 1924, were examples of this new stature. But the prophetic gifts of Cripps and of White were perhaps too strong for either the Government or for the more timid members of the Missionary Conference to countenance. On the Government's proposal to limit the rights of the African clergy, Arthur Cripps had risen up like a prophet and denounced it. The Conference backed Cripps's resolution with John White's second in a matter in which the State proposed to invade their religious realm, but when at a later Conference (1930), John White gave a paper on infringements of justice which the Native suffered in the Rhodesian Court system, the unity disappeared and White's dream of this Conference as an instrument to speak for the politically inarticulate African faded. White was not reappointed to the Executive Committee at the S.R.M.C. in 1930 and he left the meetings, convinced that his leadership had been repudiated.

12

'Flaming Indiscretions' and a Crucial Decision

In 1922 Cripps's friend, Bishop Frank Weston of Zanzibar, having won his battle for the Kenya Africans on the matter of forced labour, was walking his vast mainland East African mission circuit again. He writes of it:

> I've just done a tour of my diocese—18 months—I've walked a thousand miles since 15 December not in a purple cassock like His Amplitude of——the dear man, but in khaki shorts with a red shirt hanging down outside them—truly episcopal—in the somewhat *late* sub-apostolic manner! (ibid., p.276).

In October 1924, he was on journey again, staying in the homes of African clergy and teachers, eating their food with his fingers out of a common dish, and marching along in carpet slippers whenever his boots gave way. An infected carbuncle swept him to a swift death—and Cripps's friend and exemplar was gone.

What he meant to Arthur Cripps who, in a way, had followed his fellow-Franciscan friend of Oxford days in committing himself to Africa, and whose African experience had shown so many parallels to his own, may be indicated by the poem Cripps wrote in memory of Frank Weston and which Maynard Smith placed opposite to his own Preface in his biography of Frank Weston. In a letter later, Maynard Smith confided to Cripps that the Dean of Canterbury had declared Cripps's poem to be the finest thing in the book.

Whence was his Faith? A rushing mighty wind
First hurled her fierce infections among men....
But we, innoculating heart and mind
With spilth of pulpit and with spray of pen,
Shiver immune from Faith's contagion,....
Not so he served. For him Emmanuel glowed
In gleaming Hosts: in faces dark and wild
The Burning Babe of Bethlehem on him smiles:
The Christ, Faith hides from us, to him she showed—
A Black Christ bow'd beneath a Heart-break load.

The unorthodox orthodoxy of Frank Weston throws much light
on the next period of Arthur Cripps's life. When Cripps's friend,
Maynard Smith, was gathering the material for his biography of
Weston, a letter came to him which he quoted in the *Introduction*:

We don't want to hear about the Denominational Squadron-
Leader of the Church of England, but of the real soldier-man
of flaming indiscretions, who withstood all of those who would
enslave Africa.

From the point of view of the official Church, Cripps's own
career had been full of these 'flaming indiscretions' that were often
highly embarrassing both to the Rhodesian official church authorities as well as to the SPG under whose sponsorship Cripps was
employed and received a salary. There was, for example, the
irregularity of Cripps's ownership of the farms on which much of
his special mission work was located and which gave him such an
unusual degree of independence vis-à-vis the authorities of the
Church. Then it must be admitted that he had entered into unusual financial arrangements with his African teachers. When he
had sent them away to training schools, he was generous to a
fault in supporting them, but when they returned he expected of
them something of the same unconcerned self-giving that marked
his own life. He provided for their elementary needs and met their
emergencies to his last shilling, but there was never anything
approaching a 'union scale' in his financial relationships with them.
As Cripps saw it, they were in it together, and all that he had—his
salary, his personal income, his royalties on his books, the gifts that
came to him, his land were all theirs to be shared as far as they

went, and he assumed that his colleagues might reply in kind. At times Cripps's finances were pressed close to the abyss, and in all the years after 1910 when Cripps secured his farms, there was never a time when he was not faced with deep financial harassment.

Cripps opposed the church assessments which the official Rhodesian Anglican Church had directed were to be levied on all African communicants, and felt that such a 'head tax' on Africans was the wrong way to raise funds for the Church; that the African was already harassed by the State with these compulsory levies; and that in their poverty, their contributions to the Church must be voluntary. From the very outset Cripps had been against the Church taking government subsidies for the mission schools. In the 1920s when this issue came to a head, the highly fashionable notion of grants-in-aid for mission schools had been made popular in church circles through the educational statesmanship of the American Phelps-Stokes Commission which pressed the Churches to join with Government in running the educational system for the Africans. Cripps feared that if the Church ever became dependent on these subsidies, as he knew she must swiftly do if she entered into such a contract, she would become beholden to the Government and lose her freedom to resist it on behalf of African rights in a dozen areas that had nothing to do with education. He also saw that the Church, if it were to be saddled with the vast undertaking of serving as the educational agent of the Government, would find itself drained of its energy for its other duties. In point of fact, the Church later discovered that this was almost precisely what had happened. The pay-roll of the Education Department of the Government might be highly convenient to the church authorities as a means of carrying their missionary salaries, but one day they might find that the Church was little more than a branch of the Civil Service and its essential role hopelessly obscured and compromised. Cripps found that subsidies for mission schools were too dangerous a government noose for the Church to place around its neck.

Another 'flaming indiscretion' of Arthur Cripps in the eyes of the Church lay in what they regarded as his highly unsound and bizarre tastes in mission church architecture and his unsatisfactory methods of building these churches out of African materials, using African workmen, and in local African ways so that they needed frequent repairs and renewal. A 1923 minute in the diocesan records notes a small loan to Cripps for the repair of the new (1919) native church, the 'Southern Cross', in Umvuma, insisting that this time it be made 'water-tight' by 'competent workmen'.

There were many more items that could be tallied up on the Bishop's list of 'troubles' with this strange prophet of the back of beyond. He only came to Synod when there were African causes which he wished to champion. His records of births, baptisms, confirmations, and marriages, left much to be desired. None ever knew the next occasion when the highest authorities of Rhodesia or Britain were going to be approached by Cripps and no one had ever remembered his asking for permission to do anything! He tried the patience of his fiery old colleague, Agnes Saunders, in more affairs than can be listed; yet he defended her rights to the limit when the church authorities tried to remove her from her work at Wreningham in 1924 over her defence of an African woman who had been accused of trying to poison her.

Then there was the whole matter of his Anglican loyalty. Devoted as he was to the Anglican Eucharist and to the great basic body of Christian tradition of which the Anglican Church was the custodian, he freely joined services with the Dutch Reformed Church and his friend, Pastor Liebenberg; he insisted that he was at heart an Evangelical and was utterly devoted to his friend, John White, the Methodist; he was so close to members of the Roman Catholic Church, to which his mother and sister were converts, that he spoke always with the deepest veneration for their witness; and he more than once declared that he was 'at heart a Quaker'! Where is there to be found provision for a greater breadth of witness than in the Church of England? But the river that has no banks is a swamp, and who could deny that Cripps had carried this ecumenical business much too far? What a difficult man!

In the light of all these irregularities, what was Arthur Cripps doing at the end of the first quarter of the twentieth century serving as an SPG missionary anyway? This question, interestingly enough, had occurred at about the same time both to Arthur Cripps and in London to the Society for the Propagation of the Gospel! As early as 1921 Bishop Beaven, with whom Cripps by this time had had more than one real brush, gives some hint of these musings on Cripps's part when he noted that 'Mr Cripps still remains in the diocese, though he sometimes talks of leaving. His kindness and sympathy know no bounds, and no needs of his people go unheeded or unhelped' (S. R. Paper, cxviii, November 1921). Cripps wrote letters to John Harris, to Bishop Charles Gore, and to others in 1924 and 1925 to beg them to see if there were any financial resources that were available to help him support his mission schools without having to resort to government subsidy. But nothing came of any of these pleas. In his growing uneasiness about his own situation, and the SPG's apparent deep displeasure at his reluctance to co-operate on the educational subsidy matter, a crisis arose in 1925-26 that finally led to Arthur Cripps's leaving Rhodesia to return to his old Trinity College living at Ford End in Essex in November 1926.

While this inward crisis was going on, Bishop Beaven decided to retire and the able and energetic Edward Francis Paget, an Oxford blue, whose father had been bishop of Oxford, was chosen to succeed him. Cripps was as plain-spoken as ever while the preselection process of choosing Paget was going on, protesting vehemently against what he declared amounted to an election campaign with much playing on the many qualities of physical prowess of the candidate which he declared were neither proper nor relevant. When Bishop Paget had been elected and made his initial visit to Maronda Mashanu, he laughed with Cripps over these strictures of his about the preliminaries to his election as bishop, and assured Cripps that he was completely right in what he had said. Each took the other's measure, and the years that followed were a test for each of his understanding and of the level of their Christian concern that went beyond any institutional boundaries.

When, in 1926, Cripps's actual decision was made that he should leave Southern Rhodesia and return to England, such a close friend as Edgar Lloyd saw this as a sign of instability in him. Was it, in point of fact, a loss of nerve, the desertion of a post at a critical moment, a yielding to a temptation to defect, to run away, that hangs over every man no matter at what stage of his apostolic mission, and that may haunt a sensitive writer with doubled intensity? After all, John Frederick Oberlin, the great eighteenth-century missionary apostle to a cluster of small villages in the Vosges Mountains of Alsace, who gave his name to Oberlin College in the U.S.A., all but left his critical post there to come to America to undertake the more romantic task of missionizing the American Indians, and was only kept at his Vosges post by the outbreak of

the Revolutionary War in 1775. Perhaps the greatest Roman Catholic spiritual flame of the nineteenth century, the Curé d'Ars, to
whose confessional men and women of every station in France were
drawn, would periodically run away from the nineteen-hour-a-day
slavery to his duty in this wooden box, only to be sent after and
brought back by some parishioner in the village of Ars. Even
Livingstone in a critical moment early in his career was greatly
lured to leave the African complications behind and to ask for a
transfer to China! Was Cripps, in this fifty-seventh year of his
life, gripped irresistibly by some parallel to the death instinct that
seems to dwell in the heart of every man, even at high points in
his life, and which like an invisible hand seeks to draw him away
from that to which his life destiny is pointing? These are not idle
questions for Cripps either at this 1926 crisis or in the decade that
followed it.

The evidence, though always haunted by this shadow of defec-
tion, seems to point to something more positive, however impractical its programme of accompaniment may have been. Caught
in this vice of deep differences with regard to the whole missionary
programme that he was being asked to carry out, should he con-
form to the diocesan plans or should he take desperate measures
to get out of these toils and perhaps to end with a more radical
apostolate to the Africans than anyone had yet attempted in quite
this stark simplicity? Should he do this by resigning his SPG post
and his diocesan charge of the vast mission network and ultimately
withdraw within his own farm area where his mission stations of
Maronda Mashanu and Zuwa Rabuda were located? Meanwhile
should he try either to find or to earn in England enough money
to enable him to return and live a greatly simplified life as a
religious servant in this much narrower orbit?

One of the most convincing clues that point to this decision
being made in order to make possible a more radical apostolate was
an article on Frank Weston that Cripps wrote in 1928 as a part of
his series on *Missionary Heroes and Heroines*. In it is a challenge
that had obviously haunted Cripps since it had come to him in this
burst of confidence that Bishop Weston had made to him in his
letter in 1920:

I sometimes feel inclined to resign and live my own life with
my own children as a fellow-Christian ... for after all it is what

we are and the ideal we follow that makes our real contribution
to the world's redemption: not what we say or write or protest!
[Cripps continues in his own words]. Is not any lover of Africa
willing for Christ's sake and the Gospel's, to choose the path that
Frank Weston has indicated? Will not any European Missionary
give up his official status, and set himself to live as a fellow-
Christian among his African friends? (*G. F. S. Workers' Journal*,
(November 1928), pp.186 ff).

Without knowing quite how he would be able to manage it, Cripps
seemed to have meant to answer this question with a personal
affirmative some two years before he asked it in this article. Letters
that Cripps wrote to Harris and to Father Andrew in 1926 and
1927 would seem to confirm this view that he regarded this period
in Britain as a time of raising funds to keep his commitments to
students whom he had sent to Waddilove and to support the
religious and educational work on his farms. There is also every
indication that he intended to return to Southern Rhodesia as
soon as he could, and in this freer role which his departed friend,
Frank Weston, had suggested. He wrote a card to Bishop Paget on
18 January 1927, suggesting that he hoped to return to his own
farms 'in some very humble Evangelical capacity next year, God
enabling me'. (P.C.)

Cripps's decision to take the decisive step to leave Rhodesia and
return to a post in England was made finally during his furlough
in England in the first six months of 1926. He had already written
a long poem 'Judas Maccabeus' and submitted it for the Oxford
prize for a poem on a sacred subject, and repeated his triumph of
1902 by winning again. His friend, the poet Laurence Binyon,
wrote him late in the year on 12 December 1926, 'I'm afraid I never
thanked you for your Prize Poem *Judas Maccabeus*. I thought it
very good indeed and well sustained. Some stanzas seemed to me
to have wonderful directness and force'. (R.C.) He had left his
old friend, Mary Prior, in charge of his schools during the furlough, and practically all of his SPG salary, of some £16 a month,
which was still coming to him, had been assigned 'to help keep
things going in Mashonaland'.

It is clear that Arthur Cripps had been casting about in England
for some way to earn money to meet his obligations in Rhodesia.
He discovered that his old Trinity College living at Ford End,

which was now worth £400 a year, was falling vacant, and that both the College and the Bishop would readily reappoint him to it. He decided to accept the post. He was already committed to return to Rhodesia for the Missionary Conference at the end of July 1926, and he would at any rate need to put his house in order there for the future, so he promised to return to Britain in time to be officially installed at Ford End by 1 December 1926.

Bishop Paget was also in England at the time he received word of Arthur Cripps's decision. His reply written from Oxford on 3 July 1926 (R.C.) is revealing of their relationship:

The Church out there can ill afford to lose men of your experience and devotion. It is a loss to the country at large, both native and European.... I would like you to feel that if at any time you long for Southern Rhodesia, you will have in me a brother ready to welcome you back.

During my short stay in the Diocese I have learned to realize what your work means to the Church and to the Country; and I often wondered whether you realize to the full your influence and power today, not only in the Councils of the Church, but in the government of the land; and the respect that you and your opinions have won. However there it is...

Ever yours gratefully, Edward, Southern Rhodesia

Cripps returned to Rhodesia on the *Kildonian Castle* and landed in Cape Town 27 July 1926. Before sailing he had also laid this land issue before Professor Gilbert Murray of Oxford and had once again been invited to 'cross the river to Lambeth' to see the Archbishop of Canterbury in order to post him on the Rhodesian situation.

From the home of old Bishop Gaul, which was always his stopping place in Cape Town, Arthur Cripps posted a letter back to Bishop Paget in England suggesting his own timetable and inquiring about the Bishop's plans. 'I suppose I may have about three months in Mashonaland this time (*D.V.*) and may leave again by All Saints' Day. Are you likely to be back again by that date or are you not leaving England until late October?' (P.C.) He also sent a letter to Brother Chad which implied that negotiations were already on foot to get the old Franciscan brotherhood that J. H.

Adderley had founded, the Society of the Divine Compassion, to consider sending several of their brothers to Rhodesia to take over the diocesan end of Cripps's work in Charter District.

Cripps managed to get to Salisbury in time for the Missionary Conference and to take an active part in its proceedings. The following weeks in Charter District were strenuous and painful ones for Cripps. There were the plans to be made for the conduct of the schools on his own farms, for Cripps had no intention of turning these over to the diocese. Mary Prior agreed to move to Maronda Mashanu and to take on the oversight of this work, and Cyprian Tambo, who was now back from his years of schooling at Waddilove, had agreed to teach at the school at Zuwa Rabuda and to live there and look after this farm.

The Governor, Sir John Chancellor, had written him, 12 September 1926:

Many thanks for your letters on the land question and on juvenile employment ... I am very sorry to learn that you are leaving Rhodesia. I do not know when you propose to depart but I hope you will be able to stay a day or two with us at Government House before you go (R.C.).

Cripps was installed once more as vicar in Ford End by the Bishop of Chelmsford on the first day of December, some twenty-six years after he had left the parish late in 1900. Edgar Lloyd, who had accused him of leaving at the very moment when he was most needed in Rhodesia, wrote to Cripps on 29 December 1926, about an interim person who might settle in Wreningham until the matter of the coming of the Anglican Franciscan brothers was finally accomplished. He told Cripps that he believed some very 'regular' type of person was the sort that was needed. 'I don't suppose that either are quite our sort ... When has the irregular ever done more than to tolerate the regular and vice versa—but each is necessary for the other.' (R.C.) Cripps, for better or for worse, was now as Gòd's 'irregular' back in an earlier stall, but there was little indication that he intended to remain in this stable any longer than he could help.

Cripps's family was delighted at his return to England. His beloved niece, Elizabeth Cripps, in writing to her Aunt Edith in Torquay on 13 December 1926, says she is 'glad to hear that Arthur is fixed up all right at Ford End,' and not reckoning sufficiently with the rhythms of an 'irregular', predicts that 'possibly he will settle down after a time and become a model vicar' (R.C.).

13

Essex Again

Arthur Cripps did not move into the Ford End vicarage when he returned to his old Trinity College living in Essex but marked the ample building for use as a clubhouse for those in need. Instead he took a bed-sitter in a parishioner's house in the village and settled in where he could carry on his writing and serve the parish as its priest. But the echoes of Rhodesia were not to be stilled. His old friends could not hide how much they missed him and how much they needed him down there. Edgar Lloyd wrote Cripps on 21 January 1927, 'I think it likely you left at a critical time when a real knowledge and a poet's name and art was about to be needed' (R.C.).

Miss Brock, the head nurse at the hospital in Enkeldoorn, wrote on 12 December 1926, 'We still miss you very much. I somehow can't get used to feeling that you are so far away. It is miserable sometimes. Are you very happy at home once more?' (R.C.) On 2 January 1927, John White wrote to him:

God is very patient and compassionate or he would have long ago dismissed me from His service. I do want to serve him and native Africa with more devotion and more selflessness in 1927. Please pray for me. So much to do. So short, the time ... we miss you very much. Yours is the gift of knowing what is on the other side of the hill ... God bless you, old friend, in your parish work. Yours affectionately (R.C.).

The three and a half years that Cripps spent in the second round of Ford End were to be full of this same Rhodesian echo. Even his literary production which was not small in these years was intimately connected with Rhodesia. There was always the money needed to support his Mashonaland obligations and he toiled without interval to fashion literary projects that would help him to earn enough to meet these, both for now and for the future. Some of the writing projects that he tried to work out with the SPCK. did not materialize, but in the single year of 1928, they published under the imprint of the Sheldon Press (used for non-religious publications and school textbooks) *Chaminuka, the Man whom God Taught, Lion Man, Africans All,* and *St Perpetua, Martyr of Africa. Lion Man* had a fair sale and was a moving story of a man's possession by the spirit of the beast and of his being finally cleansed of this possession by the exorcizing power of a burst of Easter faith.

Africa for Africans, which appeared in 1927, was Arthur Cripps's message to the people of Britain about the land needs of Rhodesia's Africans, and both its text and its copious appendixes were in essence a 'White Book' in defence of a generously conceived division of the unassigned land in support of a Native Purchase Area programme.

It is interesting to find Cripps's old friend, Maynard Smith, the church historian, turning his critical powers on Cripps's book. On 31 October 1927, Maynard Smith wrote to Cripps:

Again I have been reading *Africa for Africans....* I am against a policy of segregation (which the Native Purchase Areas scheme conceded in accepting the giving up of Article 43 in the Constitution) ... If the African is, as I believe, potentially the equal of the white, he must learn to take his place with the white. Today if you lock him up in a big reserve, he would regard it as a prejudice; tomorrow he would regard it as a prison. By keeping the races apart, you make the Colour-Bar permanent ... I feel the right policy is to educate the black man to become a full citizen. Help him to do this and he will vindicate his rights for himself. He must win. Numbers are on his side ... If the African is what you take him to be, he will prove himself among white men (R.C.).

Maynard Smith's view was repudiated by Cripps at the time but interestingly enough, before Cripps died, he instructed Leonard Mamvura, his most trusted African companion, to insert a typewritten statement in each of the last six copies of this book which were to be sold by the SPCK in 1950. The statement was dated 11 July 1950 and read as follows:

Note on Segregation by A. S. Cripps: When I wrote this book, which was published in 1927, I was willing to approve of Segregation for Africans and Europeans—if Africans should be given a fair share of the land in the Colony. But afterwards I did not consider that Africans, in my opinion, were given a fair share in the S. Rhodesian Scheme of Land Apportionment, and lost my faith in Segregation for S. Rhodesia.

I am thankful for Segregation as planned by the Morris-Carter Commission for opening the way for Africans to purchase plots of land but I do not believe that Segregation is a righteous policy for a British Colony. Can it be a right policy for Christian people? Certainly not! A. S. Cripps

In the touching letters that Arthur Cripps sent almost daily to his sister 'Yuds' (Edith) in the first Essex weeks, there are records of the complexity of re-entering an English parish. Cripps was now 58 years old. In the chill Christmas weather he had some flare-ups of his old malaria, but he reports to his sister in early January that 'I am nicely free from fever today'.

Cripps was in close touch with John White and with John Harris, and the hours and days that he spent in the years from 1927 to 1930 as almost an unofficial ambassador in Britain for African interests in Rhodesia would defy calculation. He took the *Rhodesian Herald* and was able to follow minutely all that was happening in high places in Salisbury and to keep John Harris and the A.P.S. informed. He wrote from time to time in the *Manchester Guardian* or *The Times*. Cripps by now was quite at home in the matter of visiting members of the House of Commons and even managed an interview with Lady Astor. He had also taken up the Native Affairs Bill and John White had persuaded the Executive Committee of the Missionary Conference in Salisbury to pass a strong resolution against it as 'unBritish and retrograde'. John White confided to Cripps that none of the missionaries at the meeting had even read it until Cripps's letter about it appeared in the press! Cripps supplied an article, *A New Native Affairs Act in Southern Rhodesia*, for the *Contemporary*, and copies of this were generously distributed in the House. Harris wrote Cripps on 7 December 1927:

The House is very uneasy on the matter. Mr Baldwin yesterday made the important announcement that certain parts of the

Control Bill (Native Affairs Bill) are to be altered. Not only so but he has practically committed the House to a discussion before our approval is given to 'Control'.

A month later Harris wrote, 'Mr Baldwin is so disturbed about the Native Control Bill that he has sent it back [to Rhodesia] to be remodelled'.

Meanwhile, with Frank Noble, a prominent Methodist missionary in Rhodesia taking a sharply critical position towards John White in his open attempts to defend the Africans' interest in these pieces of legislation, John Harris sent to the *Methodist Times* in Britain a letter that would let them see what John White's brave championship of the African meant to the situation. John White replied:

Your article in the *Methodist Times* is altogether too generous ... My efforts on behalf of these black peoples have been very fitful ... Cripps is different. He has the soul of a great prophet, an Amos, if you like, and the tenacity of a bull-dog. He never lets go, once he grips. I am very thankful that you said these things of him.

A week earlier, 11 December 1927, John White had replied to a letter of Cripps's who had been cautioning him about looking after his health, and the letter indicates something of the tender concern for each other which these two old comrades had:

So you think I ought to go carefully for the sake of the Cause in which we are waging a warfare of sorts. What of yourself? You slog away doing the work of two men and without a thought for your own health. This I protest with the utmost sincerity! I might drop out tomorrow and there are half a dozen men who could step into my place ... But God has brought you to this task and endowed you with altogether exceptional gifts. There is not another living person could do what you are doing. I am by no means alone in thinking this. So when you preach to J. W. put in a shot for A. S. C.

Cripps had cabled his good wishes to his friend, John White, upon the occasion of his second Presidential Address to the

S.R.M.C. that was held in April of 1928. Other city officials had strongly criticized the Salisbury Mayor's action in boycotting the occasion and had been present, but it was clear that official Salisbury found the vigorous representation of African interests by the Missionary Conference less and less to its taste.

The Native Affairs Bill was finally officially sanctioned by the Secretary of State in Britain as was eventually the Bill to implement the Native Land Commission's recommendations. This only confirmed the earlier prediction that the invoking of the Royal Veto on Southern Rhodesian legislation dealing with Native affairs would be reserved for the most extreme occasions. The existence of the Veto power, however, posed a threat, and the certainty that each Bill dealing with African affairs was to be subject to full scrutiny and examination in the House of Commons, together with the fact that it might be returned to Salisbury for reformulation, gave to this Constitutional provision a certain influence on the way legislation would be drafted in the future. The continual attempts that were to be made in the next two decades by Rhodesian authorities to get this Royal Veto on legislation affecting African affairs removed from the Southern Rhodesian Constitution is some indication of the Southern Rhodesian Government's recognition of this power as being neither entirely unworkable nor completely inoperative. And the vigilance of this tiny but concerned team of Christian actionists had played no small role in these initial years of testing its functioning.

Cripps's beloved nephew, Hilary Armsrong, was in those days an undergraduate at Cambridge, not far to the north of Ford End. He recalls with what delight he occasionally came down for a week-end with his fascinating uncle, and how they often took long walking sprees together. He also remembers the wonderfully festive meals to which his uncle would take him at some inn where he would insist that he have the best beef dinners while his chivalrous old uncle would sit by and glow at his appetite, taking very little himself. Hilary Armstrong was greatly drawn to Rhodesia and after taking first-class honours at Cambridge was much tempted to join his uncle in Enkeldoorn, but this did not materialize. They remained close correspondents, however, as long as Arthur Cripps lived, and when this nephew was converted to Roman Catholicism, Arthur Cripps was completely understanding and accepting of the move.

There is little more to tell about the swiftly passing years of this Essex interlude in Cripps's life. Early in 1930 Arthur Cripps decided that he must now reurn to Rhodesia. Essex was as beautiful as ever and he managed to put together a number of his verses in praise of this favourite county into a little farewell pamphlet called *Some Essex Verses*. There were again farewell parties for Cripps at Ford End and appreciative tributes in the local papers to this true friend of Essex.

When all the festivities were over and Cripps had left Ford End for his sister Edith Cripps's home at Torquay to bid her goodbye, he found himself so strapped for funds that he could not turn up enough to pay for a third-class passage to Cape Town. He had come to Britain three-and-a-half years before to shore up his resources, to try to clear his farms of debt, and to provide enough over and above this to permit him to return on an independent basis. For henceforward there was to be no passage money, and no £16 a month from the SPG to supplement his own minute income that was now paid to him in half-yearly instalments under his mother's trust; and waiting for him in Maronda Mashanu, he knew well enough, was a nest of demands that would never let him rest.

His family's love for him had been tried for so long by his bottomless African obligations that they had long since given up. His sister Edith could not fathom her precious brother's 'restlessness' that was now driving him back to Rhodesia again when there was not so much as the faintest hint of either employment or even a licence to preach. If he would only sell his Rhodesian farms, return to England, and now, at 61, be content to live a quiet life in charge of some small parish! But one could do nothing with Arthur or with his inward yearnings. He finally managed to extract a payment from his trust, and leaving Edith with some manuscripts that he hoped might, if suitably placed, have a fair chance of bringing in some small royalties to help him, he shipped once again for Cape Town and Rhodesia.

The tall, gaunt figure of Cripps, shabbily dressed in khaki but wearing an ancient clerical collar and smoking a pipe as always was seen walking his old Charter District paths by early August 1930. He found that Cyprian Tambo had carried out his teaching and his general stewardship handsomely. ('Cyprian seems to have worked nobly here') and for the first months of his return, Cripps decided to settle with him at Zuwa Rabuda. His letters to John White and to his brother, William, give a fairly full picture of the next four-and-a-half critical years when he is trying to find whether this dream of living quietly on his own farms and sharing the life of his fellow Africans is a Christian witness that he can manage. He arrived with no assurances whatever that he would even be permitted to carry on his religious duties as an Anglican priest, although the Bishop's letter at the time of his leaving Rhodesia for Ford End had promised a warm welcome, should he ever be drawn to return. But it seems clear that he went straight ahead without any apparent hesitation.

A letter to his brother reports both some daily trekking and the making of a 'fair copy' of his Elizabethan novel, *An Outlaw in Essex*, which ran to some 50,000 words. By 2 September 1930, a letter to William speaks of a longer trek, a visit with a Paramount Chief to whom he is close, and concludes with a significant sentence, 'I had a service here this morning but outside the church, as becomes an outcast in Israel'. It would seem that he had still not consulted the Bishop about his status as far as entering into the Anglican community proper and being permitted to take services at will. On 14 November 1930, in a further letter to William, he apparently answers his brother's questioning:

> No, I'm not attached to any Mission though I've been preaching in two churches called Zuwa Rabuda (on Farm Moneyputt, where I live), and Maronda Mashanu (on Farm Muckleneuk) which is about three miles nearer to Enkeldoorn. No, I don't get any salary from any Mission, though Bishop Paget of 'Southern Rhodesia', the Anglican Diocese here, seems inclined to be friendly (R.C.)

The plain facts of the matter were that Arthur Cripps did not wish to ask for a licence from the Bishop. To do so would have been to put himself under the Bishop's authority. He felt that this would involve him in the 'Church of the Province of South Africa' and its willingness to accept grants from the government which for Cripps meant coming under the thumb of the 'Granting Authority' —the State. Cripps hoped that his original ordination and his status as a retired priest of the Church of England might be enough, and he more than once in his later years followed his name with the designation, 'Clerk in Holy Orders'.

Archbishop Paget, as he had become when he wrote a personal letter to me on 18 September 1963, had this to say about Cripps's precise clerical status in the post-1930 years:

He always refused a licence from the Bishop because the Church received Government grants for the African Schools but he and I remained close friends and I always treated him as a priest of the Diocese. When he went to Ford End (1926) I persuaded him to hand over to the Diocese all the work in the All Saints, Wreningham, district, i.e., in and around Enkeldoorn, except the work on his own farms during his absence. On his return he (eventually) went to live on his farm at Maronda Mashanu— the Mission of the Five Wounds; and I always confirmed any candidates prepared by him, either in his Mission or at All Saints', Wreningham ... He built and paid for the Church of the Five Wounds and many other churches in that district.

Perhaps this letter, as well as a conversation which I once had with Archbishop Paget in which he shook his head and laughed about Cripps's irregularity and said that he had been very glad to overlook it, adding, 'I think I know a saint when I see one, and I just let him alone!' says as much about the quality of Archbishop Paget as it does about the ecclesiastical status of Cripps! The only comment of the Bishop which was inserted in the minutes of the 1930 Diocesan Synod that was held shortly before Cripps's return was, 'The Rev. A. S. Cripps is about to return to the Diocese but does not desire to accept a licence and pay, and therefore there will be no liability to the Provincial Pension Fund on his behalf'.

In no time at all, the irregular but completely accepted Arthur Cripps was swept into the heart of the religious work of the Charter District. The Society of the Divine Compassion was of course in charge, but the jurisdictional lines were not easy to draw when the old man was available. Cripps was used to living in the Providence of God and took what life brought him. The Africans called on him for baptism, for weddings, for funerals, for visiting their sick, and performing all of those Christian duties which are detailed so pointedly in Matthew 25, and he responded. He was drawn in to take services for colleagues who were ill, for Father Andrew, for Edgar Lloyd, and for others. There was the call of visiting the prisoners in the Enkeldoorn gaol or the sick in the hospital, and his older white friends in the community often begged for his private ministrations, and he gave them. Then there was always the special responsibility for serving the two churches on his farms. These needed not only spiritual nurture, but Maronda Mashanu required attention to the very building itself. In 1931 and again in 1933 he reports giving much personal work in the roofing of the Maronda Mashanu church building and speaks of the generous gift of excellent roofing poles from the farm of his friend, the Charter District Native Commissioner, J. W. Posselt.

After a few months of living at Zuwa Rabuda, he had returned to his small rondavel at Maronda Mashanu and he continued to live there until his death in 1952. The next year, the Bishop invited him to attend his Retreat, but Cripps, although touched by his kindness, politely declined the invitation. He managed to prepare two position papers for the 1932 Southern Rhodesian Missionary Conference, presenting them *in absentia*, for since he was no longer an official priest of the diocese, he did not feel eligible to attend the meeting. Perhaps there was even more to it than that. With his deep loyalty to John White, Cripps found it hard to forgive the Conference for removing his comrade from the Executive Committee in 1930 and taking the more cautious way. On 25 August 1930, Cripps wrote a comforting letter to John White, whom he always referred to as the 'Apostle of Mashonaland':

> Your splendid but sad little letter came back to me from England. You say, 'My reputation, I fear, is gone in missionary circles', and yet Laurence, S.D.C., seems to think that you, John White, were the best man at that Conference in Bulawayo, and when I alleged your sanctity to Burbridge (S.J.) I gathered that even his authoritative mind assented (J.W.).

But his feelings of the wrong that had been done to John White could not be suppressed.

Cripps wrote his brother William on 5 October 1930, 'I stayed 3 nights and Mr and Mrs White were so kind. What a fine Crusade J. W. has been putting up for the Black Christ. The Missionaries have not re-elected him to their Executive Committee'. (R.C.) When C. F. Andrews's book on John White appeared in 1935, two years after John White's death, Cripps's anger over what had happened to his friend in 1930 was kindled again. Frank

Noble, the leading Methodist clergyman who had not come off too well in C. F. Andrews's description in the biography of White that depicts the 1928-30 years of John White's leadership of the Missionary Conference, demanded an opportunity in any future edition of the book to rewrite the chapter describing this period. In a letter to Frank Mussels, who had assembled the materials from which Andrews had written the book, Cripps, on 29 May 1935, wrote:

About the suggestion of the Rev. Frank Noble for the rewriting of the history of J. White's relations with the Missions Conference toward the end of his life—please pass on word to him [C. F. Andrews] that if he should agree to print a brief statement of F. Noble's point of view as to those relations in any future edition of *John White of Mashonaland* that may be called for, I want him to agree to print a brief statement of A. Cripps's point of view also.

Cripps goes on in the letter to deal with the various excuses that were made about dropping White from the Executive when he was at the height of his powers, and then comes back to what he believes to be the real reason for their action, namely, White's 1930 paper on 'Rhodesia's Judicial System' in which he pinpointed examples of the unfair legal treatment the Africans were receiving at the hands of the Rhodesian police officials and the courts:

Did one single Missionary Conference member stand up and say a word on his behalf when Mr Leggate saw fit to trounce him for speaking out boldly against a Public Evil—the Extortion of Evidence? Fauh! The mangy forcible-feeble crowd! *Truth is great and will prevail*, yes, in spite of that skilful ecclesiastical casuist, who was not able as he so engagingly and amiably admits himself, to persuade John White to replace a frontal attack policy by diplomatic action (J.W.).

There was, however, more at stake in this defence than simply White's honour. For in the closing line of this letter the frontal attack issue is cited on which Cripps believed the Missionary Conference had foundered in 1930. And it is interesting to see his opinion championed by a paper on *State and Church in Southern Rhodesia 1919-39* (Historical Association of Rhodesia and Nyasa.

Local Series 4-6) by a young historian, T. Ranger, who sums up his own thesis at the outset:

> It is the argument of this paper that Cripps and White did comprehend the essentials of the position and that their policy (of vigorously and openly defending the Africans' interests in a period when he was unable to do this for himself) was the best suited to the circumstances, and that their failure was a tragedy for the Church of South Africa (p.8).

In leading the Missionary Conference to place itself within Rhodesia on the side of the poor and the inarticulate, where the Christ of any generation hides himself, and in this instance, therefore, on the side of the African; and to seek to awaken the conscience of white Rhodesia to its responsibility for dealing fairly with the less fortunate 19/20ths of its population, these two stalwarts, Cripps and White were bound together. Their friendship showed itself in moving ways in the next three years, as John White battled with cancer and lost.

14

God's Irregular

When Arthur Shearly Cripps knew why John White had asked
the Methodist Church to release him in 1932, it was as if a sentence
had been passed on his own life as well. For White was his con-
fidant and there was nothing in the cause for which Cripps lived
that they would not dare to undertake together. Now Cripps was
faced with going it alone and he knew well enough his own
terrible inadequacies. Until now, John White had been not only
his companion, counsellor, and comforter, but he had been able to
take the prophetic ideas of his fiercely individualistic and irregular
friend and to implement them in the public arena of the clerical
group or the national scene where John White, for all of his recent
troubles, had been a natural leader of men. John White could and
did go out to an annual meeting of the Rhodesian Agricultural
Union and take on the white farmers in a discussion. Cripps would
only have courted a lynching from such a company. For John White
on the other hand, Cripps was his relentless Maronda Mashanu
conscience walking again and again the seventy-five miles out to
Waddilove and the seventy-five miles back, to goad him to continue
the battle for their cause. He knew that Cripps as a lone Franciscan
was able to share the Africans' poverty as he had never done. Edgar
Lloyd met this difference by deriding the Franciscan way as too
extreme, or in pointing out to Cripps how utterly un-Franciscan
he was in argument or in judgement. But for John White, he knew
the cost of what Cripps was about and he took off his shoes in
his presence. David and Jonathan could hardly have been more
closely bound together than these two.

John White finally agreed to surgery and Mr Huggins (later, Sir
Godfrey Huggins) operated on him in Salisbury. This was followed
by an apparent recovery, but then came a relapse. There was a
brave scene where John White, already weak with his trouble,
insisted upon coming by car to Enkeldoorn in order to pay one

more visit to his treasured friend and to participate in an ecumenical service which Cripps had arranged in the Dutch Reformed church.

Cripps made pilgrimages to the hospital in Salisbury and then finally to John White's home at Maswingo to take final leave of his friend before White left for Britain. He joined with Frank Mussels in urging White to give them the joy and enlightenment that would come from the writing of his reminiscences of his Rhodesian term of service that had begun in 1894. The Whites settled near Birmingham, England, and letters between Cripps and White were exchanged almost every week until the end.

Late in 1932, John White met C. F. Andrews, and Andrews was to become for him almost a spiritual brother and chaplain in the remaining months of his life. C. F. Andrews was on leave from India that year and held the Woodbrooke Fellowship which permitted him to live at Woodbrooke, the Quaker Religious Centre at Selly Oak on the outskirts of Birmingham, and to have the rare indulgence of a time of freedom to write. His *Christ in the Silence*, which was dedicated to John White, was written during that winter of 1932-33 and C. F. Andrews insisted that it could never have been managed if he had not been privileged to share the closing days of this great spirit's life. John White died on 10 August 1933, and his ashes were taken back to Rhodesia and buried near the Maswingo African School which he had founded. Cripps walked from Maronda Mashanu to Maswingo to kneel at this grave, and then walked quietly home again. One hundred and fifty miles of foot slogging gave him time to think, to thank, and to resolve. Out of the visit came his poem, 'John White's Grave', and under the title is a verse from the eleventh chapter of Amos, 'Behold I am pressed under you, as a cart is pressed that is full of sheaves'. The poem is one of the few memorial verses that Cripps chose to include in his *Africa: Verses*. In its verses are the lines:

> He is not here. By rough roads he
> Rode transport to Eternity:
> Heap'd high with sheaves 'twas his to come—
> Like farmer's cart—to Harvest Home:
> Press'd as with bronze-brown sheaves, they strain'd—
> Those creaking wheels—ere Home was gain'd......

Of all the graves in this great land
This is the one her God has plann'd
For Africa's abiding bliss—
This find-and-follow grave of his.

(pp.49-50).

In the year that followed John White's death, C. F. Andrews
was persuaded by Frank Mussels to take what there were to John
White's own reminiscences and the materials that he had collected
about John White, including eight long memoranda which Arthur
Cripps had poured out, giving his memories of their long friendship and of their struggles together for African rights, and from
these papers to prepare a biography of John White. There was a
wonderful gathering in Selukwe in 1934 when, as the guests of
the Mussels, Cripps and C. F. Andrews spent a week-end together
and discussed the details of the biography. It appeared in 1935
under the title of *John White of Mashonaland*. C. F. Andrews
dedicated the volume to Arthur Shearly Cripps and included in it
a chapter on Cripps which was largely drawn from John White's
notes. Cripps, when he discovered the dedication, wrote to his
brother of the 'book about Alexander-the-Great dedicated to Alex-
ander-the-copper-Smith', (R.C.) but the tribute was not lost on
the grieving Cripps. The biography had about it the skill of an
accomplished writer but it lacked the firm touch of an intimate
knowledge of Rhodesia itself. Of the reviews, Victor Murray's
seemed to have sensed the situation most perceptively when he
referred to the book as savouring more of the Johannine tradition
than of that of Mark!

There had been something very steadying about this friendship
with John White that ran like a thread through the vast unsettle-
ment in Arthur Cripps in these first years of his return to Rhodesia.
He had no hesitation, for instance, about sharing with White his
attraction towards Roman Catholicism which had always been
present, but which in this time of return and uncertainty had apparently become especially acute. His sister Edith had written to
William Cripps on 13 July 1929, 'He [Arthur] sometimes talks
about being a Catholic but I do not think he will...' Was it by
accident that he made his early visit to Father Burbridge as he
re-entered Rhodesia in 1930?

There had sprung up in South Africa under the leadership of

C. Kadalie, an African, a kind of Christian Socialist African trade
union which called itself the Independent Industrial Christian
Union and had made some vigorous moves in South Africa to
assert African rights. Cripps knew and admired Kadalie and had
corresponded with him. In Cripps's English interlude, Kadalie had
sought to get the I.C.U. established in Rhodesia, and on Cripps's
return this seemed to him a most promising vehicle. In letters of
7 October and 28 October 1930, he had gone so far with John White
as to raise the issue of their joining. 'As to I.C.U., may it not
be that the I.C.U. may be chosen to take that protagonist's place
in our Crusade from which the Interdenominational Missionary
Conference by its rejection of your service in its Exec. etc. has been
abdicating?' And in the next letter he asks, 'But when are you and
I going to throw ourselves into the Ind. I.C.U. not counting the
cost in one way but counting it in another!!! May God guide us!!!'
(J.W.) Apparently one of the costs that he faced was Father Burbridge's displeasure at a clergyman joining anything so radical in
character. In an earlier letter, dated 6 October 1930, Cripps had
told White, 'I suppose if I join I.C.U. for which I seem to be
eligible, Burbridge may interpret it as an act of defiance'. (J.W.)
By 3 November 1930, he wrote to White, referring to himself

> as one who in spite of all of his anti-clericalism, loves and
> reveres the Old Church for what it has done to keep the His-
> torical Christian Creed and the Tradition of Christian Morals
> inviolate throughout the ages. Deo Gratias!!! When Father
> Kaignault, s.j., said mass in the Enkeldoorn Hospital stoep last
> week, I knelt with Catholic Africans outside and below. But as
> you may guess, my attitude to the Independent I.C.U. seems
> likely to keep me away from the reception of the Roman Catholic
> Church's sacraments quite effectively, and I am surely a 'Quaker
> at heart' in my way and likely (*D.V.*) to continue so (J.W.).

On 17 November 1930, he wrote to White of preaching at Zuwa
Rabuda that morning 'about St Hugh of Lincoln who gave an
Archbishop such stern measure, who stood up to those awesome
Plantagenet Kings, and who championed the poor man so de-
votedly'. (J.W.) It is quite clear that Cripps is back in the era of the
undivided Catholic Church and trying to see his own role in the
light of strong precedents. An old Anglican friend, now turned

Roman Catholic, who is the Superior at Chishawasha, J. R. Quinn, had written to twit him on his curious ecclesiastical state of limbo, and Cripps cites the letter to White: 'You're not founding a new church are you, which you will have to hand over to the C. of E. when you die?' (J.W.) But the Roman Catholic issue was still not settled. Cyprian Tambo remembered a sixty-mile journey, each way, that Cripps made on foot in 1931 to the Jesuit Mission station at Driefontein; he recalled how he, Tambo, had reproached his Anglican Father and guide, Cripps, for going there, reminding him of how when he had sent him to Methodist Waddilove more than a decade before, he had told him that he wanted him to remain an Anglican. Now here he was going off to consult with these Roman Catholic Fathers! Cripps brushed this aside at the time, but when he returned, Tambo added, he told me that 'we would best stay where we are'.

Some reflection of this visit may be present in a letter to White of 8 April 1931 where he speaks of intending to visit Father Martindale 'to try to make an appeal to him to mediate with Roman Catholic powers-that-be in favour of a more moderate and indeed sympathetic attitude towards the young Africa movement, quoting the precedent of sympathy shown to young Ireland's aspiration' (J.W.). On 17 April he wrote to White, 'I trekked in ... and spent a night at Driefontein last week. Fathers Martindale and ——were very kind to me and charming but do not commend themselves to me altogether as to furthering of Africa's horizons'. (J.W.) This seems to end the matter in the letters of the period. Then years later, Father Burbridge in a letter to Hilary Armstrong, who had since become a Roman Catholic, remarked that his Uncle [Cripps] seemed to be further away from the Church than he had been some years before!

The naturalness of Cripps's sharing these confidences with John White does much to unravel a hidden chapter of these unsettled years of his return to Rhodesia. White had been the silent, understanding listener in whose presence Cripps had come to his decision 'to stay where we are'. If Cripps did seek for the conditions that would make the Roman Catholic sacrament available to him, his own judgement seemed to be that the price was prohibitive, since it might be acquiescing in that Church's lack, as it seemed to him, of any passionate desire for the Africans' total condition. Nor could he be a part of even so precious a company, as he ideally held his Roman Catholic brothers to be, if their concern for the Africans' future was no more kindled than he seemed to find it. He knew the Anglican frailties in this regard—but he also sensed the freedom he had in their fellowship to press the African cause.

It is interesting to speculate as to what Cripps, who found even the light hand of Anglican authority almost unbearable, would have made of the discipline under which he would have come in the Roman Catholic Church of that day. There can be little doubt, however, that the whole mystical and historical side of the Church had an almost irresistible lure for Cripps, and in these latter years of his life when he was casting about to see what his remaining calling was really intended to be, he had opened the door of his heart by a few degrees to the Church of his beloved Poverello. Though he stayed where he was, the generous and affectionate ties he had with his Roman Catholic brethren continued to the very end of his life and a number of them attended his funeral. It was as if they sensed in him one who had been authentically enough touched by the coals from the altar to be their brother, and they treated him as such. It is no longer a secret that literally all of the later ecumenical 'discoveries' were lived and practised generations before in many a pocket of the mission field. Perhaps Cripps, in his ecumenical feeling that he was already one of them in those things that really mattered, and that 'converting' back and forth was less important than their common commitment to a relentless Master, was once again a harbinger of the future.

With no clear-cut work, no salary, and pressed by the boundless needs of his African friends with whom he lived, Cripps felt that he must find some more specific task and a source of income otherwise he doubted if he could continue to live in Rhodesia. Once again he laid these matters before John White and one of the last letters, dated 22 June 1933, that White wrote to him from Britain contained a word to call him back to his vocation to 'stay where we are' in territory as well as in religious affiliation: 'I personally think there is more scope for you in Rhodesia than elsewhere' (N.A.).

Strangely enough the path of deliverance, through an urgent and very specific need requiring his attention, had already come on the scene. On 29 October 1932, the doctor at Enkeldoorn Hospital asked Cripps if a group of African venereal disease patients who required regular treatment over some consecutive weeks, might be housed on Cripps's farm at Maronda Mashanu, and if Cripps would be responsible for seeing that they appeared at the out-patient clinic at the hospital at the times appointed for treatment. The government physician promised that this would be only a temporary arrangement, since they intended to build a special wing on to the African end of the hospital to house these patients, whom they would expect to be ready to take off Cripps's hands in a matter of a very few months. On 29 October 1939, *seven year later*, Cripps wrote to his brother William that they were celebrating the seventh anniversary of the V.D. work coming to Maronda Mashanu! The depression in Rhodesia had changed hospital plans as well as those of the Native Purchase Areas and the arrangement by which Cripps was given ... £10 a month to keep these people was far too attrac-tive a way for the State to dispose of this problem to cause it, in its straitened circumstances, to take any great pains to interrupt it.

This V.D. clinic work was different from anything Cripps had undertaken before. But the need was there, the men were thankful to have such an agreeable place to stay, and in the end thankful enough, too, to be rid of the loathsome diseases they had contracted. Cripps was reasonably confident that if he did not take them on, this course of treatments which cost the State a minimum of £2 a patient before they were finished, might well be discontinued. As the years went on, he accepted it as something to which he had been called and as one of the few really personal things he could do for the African. It seems to have been a highly important in-strument in pinning him down, and in helping him to 'stay where we are'. After all, Francis, too, found Assisi more bearable when there was the leper hutch at the foot of the hill which needed daily service.

Cripps's final 'settling in' took almost five years. The V.D. clinic was a local stabilizer, but almost equally important were the growing number of matters that required Cripps's public interven-tion on the Africans' behalf. For now John White was gone, and if Cripps withdrew, who would put the African case? Perhaps the final precipitating event that concluded this process of stabilization was the death of Edith Cripps at the turn of the year 1934-5. She had had an accident which she survived by only a few days. Now Cripps's temptation to return to England to see her once more was over. He could not go home again. There was no home now to go to, for both William and Doll were engrossed in their own families.

By the middle of 1935, this wistfulness seems to have disappeared from his correspondence entirely. It might also be noted that the six years of the Second World War effectively sealed Rhodesia off from Britain as far as civilians were concerned, and by 1945 Cripps was old and blind and quite reconciled to finishing the course where he was.

15

Now is Not the Time to Rest

The Society of the Divine Compassion, which had served the Wreningham district since 1927, withdrew in 1933 some three years after Cripps's return. The Bishop, hard put as he was to find a suitable substitute, unfortunately took as an interim appointment, a white priest from Nyasaland who shall remain unnamed. He came down with his caravan car and during the period of his régime proceeded to impose what he declared to be proper order on the Anglican Mission churches of the Charter District. He insisted that individual church assessments for each African mission station be paid promptly and in full and not only did he refuse communion to any African who was behind in his dues, but he actually burned down several of the primitive mission stations which were delinquent in their assessments! These simple African buildings were not of much actual value, but Cripps and the Africans had taken some pains to see that they were erected and maintained and even though Cripps was no longer in any official post in the District, the action of the priest from Nyasaland nearly drove the mercury through the top of Arthur Cripps's thermometer.

Bishop Paget learned from Cripps of what was going on and after conducting an investigation through two of his other clergy, put a stop to it. Some time after the priest had left, the Bishop made a special trip to Charter District and went with Cripps to several of these sites where the mission building had been destroyed and in purple penitence let Arthur Cripps stand in the ashes and preach, as only a wounded prophet could, to the gathered Africans. Bishop Paget then made it doubly clear to the Africans that he did not approve of what had been done, and would help with the restoration. On this little penitential pilgrimage, Cripps accepted a lift in the Bishop's car and Paget was not above twitting him a bit about his riding in an automobile. Cripps only grinned and said gaily, 'They have their uses'.

Pastor Liebenberg died on 6 October 1933. He had been Cripps's Dutch Reformed Pastor friend through all the years in Enkeldoorn. The great Pastor Louw of the Dutch Reformed Church came to Enkeldoorn to preach the memorial sermon in the church and Arthur Cripps took the service at the grave as he had done before for two of Liebenberg's children. Cripps refused to ride in the carriage behind the body of his beloved friend, feeling that he was not worthy to do so, but ran on ahead to the cemetery and was standing at the grave when the funeral cortège arrived.

Cyprian Tambo continued to teach at Zuwa Rabuda for something over two years after Cripps returned to Rhodesia. Arthur Cripps believed that in this young man there was a true calling to the priesthood, so in 1933 he arranged with the Bishop for him to have his theological training at Penhalonga. Tambo finished there in 1937 and after passing his examinations was ordained a priest in Salisbury in 1939. Arthur Cripps, now 70 years of age, walked the 95 miles up and the 95 miles back in order to attend Tambo's ordination and always looked on Cyprian Tambo as his spiritual son.

Another African priest who was especially close to Cripps in this period was the Reverend Edward Chipunza. He was appointed to. Wreningham in 1934 after the débâcle, and served there until 1942. He and Cripps saw much of each other in those years. Chipunza recalled that even after Cripps's health had begun to fail, his wit was as sharp as ever. One day when he was jousting a little with the old Cripps, he told him a little mockingly not to worry, that he would be on hand to carry him when he died. Cripps threw back his head and said, 'You may go first!' Like so many of his fellow Africans, Chipunza revered Cripps so much that he bowed his head as he spoke of their friendship and joined the chorus in saying, 'He was a Francis of Assisi to Southern Rhodesia'.

In the matter of Cripps's public interventions on the Africans' behalf, the years from 1934-40 showed little abatement over the earlier period from 1918-30. Some of these interventions were more strictly local Rhodesian affairs. Others were Rhodesian decisions that Cripps once again ventilated before British officials, the British parliament and the British public in order to use pressure on the ultimate decision.

Sir John Harris, who had been knighted in 1933, continued to put the service of the A.P.S. at Cripps's disposal, and after 1936

Cripps developed a close relationship with Arthur Creech-Jones, an ardent Labour Party friend of the Africans, who was to become the Colonial Secretary in the Labour Government after the Second World War. Creech-Jones was associated with the Colonial Bureau of the Fabian Society with whom Cripps had an extensive correspondence from 1936-40. Other British consultants and concerned friends of this 1934-40 period were Lionel Curtis, Lord Lothian, and Margery Perham of *The Times* and later reader in Colonial Administration at Oxford. The Editor of the *Manchester Guardian* seemed to have a special partiality towards Arthur Cripps's *Letters to the Editor.*

From his remote V.D. clinic and amid his duties as a priest on his Enkeldoorn farms, Cripps continued to supply the initiative and the pulling of the alarm bell, as well as authentically investigating local and grass-roots instances and materials including a number of statements from young African leaders on what they actually saw taking place. The use of these efforts both in Rhodesia and in Britain was managed much as before.

There was no doubt that the Southern Rhodesian political leaders, now in their second decade of power, were growing increasingly confident that they could manipulate their legislation dealing with African affairs so that they would get their way in the end. They knew that Downing Street could delay and perhaps compel them to restate their formulations, but the Rhodesians sensed the British Government's reluctance to invoke the veto itself, and they traded heavily on this. On the other hand, this minimal expression of British power always had back of it the possibility of using greater power, and vigorous and informed parliamentary discussion of issues in the House of Commons or the House of Lords was a way of keeping this ultimate power of the veto from withering away to nothing. Throughout the years under scrutiny from 1934-40, Southern Rhodesia's Prime Minister, Huggins, again and again tried unsuccessfully to persuade the British authorities to permit the changing of the Rhodesian Constitution to eliminate this imperial veto on legislation dealing with African affairs. In the latter part of the next decade from 1940-50, he tried to persuade them to permit him to drop the Africans from the open franchise privilege, which because of income and property restrictions was little enough used, but which nevertheless also imposed a potential threat. Cripps's activity, therefore, was a small but not inconsequen-

tial factor in keeping alive this eternal vigilance that is the price of
preserving liberties which may vanish if they are not continually
appealed to. When the African could speak for himself, this kind
of championship might lapse. But that time had not yet come in
Rhodesia, and in spite of his age Cripps felt, as Teresa of Avila had
once declared, that 'Now is not the time to rest'.

As for some of the more strictly domestic Rhodesian issues, Cripps
wrote a pamphlet in 1934, in which he resisted sharply the effort of
a group of white phonetic linguists who were trying to intrude into
written Shona a whole new set of symbols that would tend to separate it from the stream of other African languages.

He protested strongly against action on the part of local officials
that forced Natives on the Sabi Reserve in his own Charter District
to use their own bullocks, ploughs, and hand-tools, and to work day
after day without any rationing or pay whatsoever to build roads
through the Reserve that were to be used almost exclusively by
motorized public officials. After repeated failures to secure government investigation of the affair, Cripps, in spite of warnings by a
highly placed Rhodesian official, privately published a pamphlet,
*How Roads Were Made in the Native Reserves of Charter District
Mashonaland, S.R. 1934-5.*

Later he investigated a de-stocking incident in the Fort Victoria
region where Africans were pressed by local officials to sell their
cattle to white dealers getting a price which was less than half of
what they might have expected. A packing company was involved
in the incident. Cripps succeeded in making sufficient stir over the
matter so that the Prime Minister finally was pressed into issuing
a statement that there was no law that made the Africans sell
their cattle. This statement gave something solid for the Africans
to go by and protected them from the insinuations made by local
officials that such sales were by government command.

Among the issues that Cripps took to the broader British forum,
three might be mentioned. On 25 October 1935, the Native
Preachers Bill was introduced into the Southern Rhodesian legislature. It was a stiffened-up version of one that had been withdrawn
at the suggestion of the S.R.M.C. after being proposed in 1924.
The government was still fearful that uncontrolled African preaching might be a potential source of disaffection to the government.
Cripps published a pamphlet which attacked the measure. This
was widely read in Rhodesia and spread about in Britain and

helped to mobilize criticism there. The backfire among the clergy and mission bodies both in Rhodesia and Britain was sharp enough so that once again the government withdrew the bill.

The Rhodesian government was more determined when it introduced its Native Registration Act in 1936 that went further than ever before in hampering the African's freedom of movement. It required the securing of special written passes by Africans before they could enter a town even in the daylight hours when they were accustomed to bring in their produce for sale and to make their purchases at the shops. Both Bishop Paget and Robert Tredgold, a leading barrister in Rhodesia who later entered the cabinet and then held Rhodesia's highest legal offices, denounced the act as oppressive.

Cripps sent a very full memorandum to his friend, the governor Herbert Stanley, who was on a visit to Britain asking him to show it personally to the Secretary of State for the Dominion and he received word that Stanley had been enough under the weight of Cripps's memorandum to share it with the Prime Minister Stanley Baldwin himself. Cripps had two 'Letters to the Editor' printed in the *Manchester Guardian* on 19 February 1937. Sir John Harris, and even C. F. Andrews, in response to a telegram received in India from Cripps, had also written letters that were used in the *Manchester Guardian*. Arthur Creech-Jones, who had helped mightily with the questions in the House of Commons, wrote Harris about these letters in the *Guardian*, 'It is obvious that both the Dominion and Colonial opinion is sensitive to publicity of this kind' (F.C.B.).

There was a substantial African petition against the Act that was forwarded to Britain, and Cripps saw to it that when Huggins went to Britain in the spring, he received calls from strong delegations who let him see that there was sharp disapproval of what he had done. Lord Lothian wrote that he had pleaded Cripps's cause in the House of Lords. Huggins, after a sizeable delay, had his way in the end, but at the price of wide circles in Britain being stirred by the injustice that was being imposed. Cripps wrote John Harris that gaol accommodations in Salisbury were being extended! The Native Registration Act when enforced meant for the Africans countless trips to gaol over the small irregularities that were inevitable. Arthur Creech-Jones wrote to thank Cripps for all the material on this matter that he had forwarded to him adding, 'We [the Colonial Bureau of the Fabian Society] regard you as one of our very few sources of reliable information on native affairs' (F.C.B.).

The third British effort came in 1938 when he had word from both Creech-Jones and Harris that a Royal Commission headed by Lord Bledisloe had been appointed to look into the matter of the Amalgamation of the Protectorates of Nyasaland and Northern Rhodesia and Southern Rhodesia. Both Harris and Lionel Curtis had come to Rhodesia just prior to the arrival of the Commission and Cripps had seen them and realized how much was at stake in the outcome of this Commission. Cripps was bitterly opposed to any such amalgamation and to the imposition of the racially backward standards of Southern Rhodesia on the other two essentially black territories where, with only a very small number of whites in the total population, the relations between the races were very much more relaxed. He was determined to get all of the evidence against such a proposal that he could assemble.

In addition to stirring others to testify, Cripps was himself invited to give evidence and he met the Commission on 14 June 1938. He had prepared with care a massive dossier and the first part of his testimony consisted of reading from this shrewd document. Drawing on his accurate knowledge of African taxation in Southern Rhodesia, and pointing out the passing of progressively more repressive laws limiting the African freedom in Southern Rhodesia, the unfair distribution of the land, the absence of African representation in the legislature and the exclusion of the African from the Trade Council measures, Cripps pressed the Commission to spare the Africans of Nyasaland and Northern Rhodesia the fruits of what this Amalgamation would be sure to bring.

Cripps was delighted at the Commission's report. He wrote his brother on 25 March 1939:

So that Royal Commission's Report is out! Thank God that it is apparently so definitely against any immediate idea of Amalgamation of the Northern Territories with S.R.!!!! It may surely have helped to remove a little of the whitewash off the sepulchre of Southern Rhodesia's Native Policy, may it not? (R.C.).

But he was not through with this matter of Amalgamation which for Cripps hung like a shadow over the land for all the years of the war and was finally brought into existence as the Federation of Rhodesia and Nyasaland a year after his death. He quotes to his brother in a letter of 27 January 1940, a letter on the Amalgamation issue that had come to him from Miss Margery Perham.

I think the more informed advice that can be brought to bear on the Sec. of State the better. Also the sooner the better. I can assure you I have done all I can myself. I have seen him and talked of it. These matters are all a question of the strongest pressure (R.C.).

And Cripps kept nibbling away at this issue in any way that he could until the very end of his life.

16

Does the Road Wind Up-hill
All the Way?

Although he was approaching his seventieth year, Cripps was still given to making his travels by foot, though now on occasion he was not above accepting some other form of transport when it was offered. It was in this period that the story is told of Cripps, with an African companion, being offered a lift in a car for the last leg of their ninety-five mile journey to Salisbury. Cripps accepted the offer gratefully and took his seat. But before his African friend could get in, the door was slammed shut and the car swept off. During the journey there was a polite silence and when some miles later they reached Salisbury, Cripps thanked the man for the lift and asked to be let out. The white driver asked him where he was going and Cripps said quietly that he was walking back to rejoin his African companion on their journey to Salisbury!

Late in 1938, John Snelling, a gifted young archivist in Salisbury had succeeded in publishing an attractive anthology which he called *Rhodesian Verse—1888-1938*. Snelling chose to include thirteen of Arthur Cripps's poems in this collection, almost double the number of any other author. He also persuaded Cripps, as the informal poet-laureate of Rhodesia, to write a nine-page introduction which had about it a good deal of charm.

In the following year, the Oxford University Press honoured Arthur Cripps by publishing a handsome collection of the choicest of his African poems entitled *Africa: Verses*. The book contained a prefatory note by Lord Tweedsmuir which has already been mentioned in connection with *Lyra Evangelistica*. The rest of the note reads:

This is not the place to speak of the courageous and unselfish work he has done in Africa as a pioneer missionary. I am concerned only with his poetic gift, which I think is unlike that of any other writer of today. He is a classical scholar and deeply read in the literature of the past, and now and then he seems to have affinities with the lyricists of the early seventeenth century. He has, therefore, a great tradition behind him, but he has cunningly adapted it to the needs of a new land, and for me the unique charm of his work is that he can sing the songs of Zion and at the same time give them the charm of and mystery of the Waters of Babylon.

Late in July 1939, Laurence Binyon wrote him praising the volume. In a matter of months Britain was to be engulfed in another world-shaking war, and within a year, Arthur Cripps's seemingly unshatterable physique was to reveal that it, too, was vulnerable. But for a flash in 1939, this seventieth year of his life, the sun broke through for Cripps and warmed him to the core. In the early months of the following year, three of his close friends slipped away: Lord Tweedsmuir, C. F. Andrews, and Sir John Harris, and the long loneliness of advancing age extended its borders.

Cripps himself suffered a slight stroke in early 1940 from which he made a swift recovery, but at long last he was compelled to acknowledge, ever so reluctantly, that his eyes were failing disastrously. Arthur Blaxall, who had done so much for the African blind in South Africa, had invited Cripps to come by air to Johannesburg to consult a brilliant opthamologist, Dr Boshoff, but Cripps demurred. In late March 1940, the situation worsened so much that in spite of Cripps's pleas to let him defer the matter until after his Easter religious duties were completed, he was taken to the hospital in Salisbury and on 27 March, his left eye, afflicted with an ulcerated cornea, was removed. On his return to Enkeldoorn, Diana Schultz and others tried to persuade him to be cared for in the town itself but they knew in advance the outcome. 'Our old saint is stubborn', wrote one of these women to his elder brother, William Cripps. 'As I know my friend, he will scorn these offers and stick to his beloved Maronda Mashanu', which he did.

There were various theories of how his eye had become infected—theories that ranged from his intimate touch with the V.D. clinic, or the insanitary situation in which he lived in this small African hut at Maronda Mashanu, to the long night vigils of reading and writing with only a candle for light, or almost the precise opposite, the fierce glare of the Rhodesian sun that he faced in his long years of foot-slogging. The purpose of removing the left eye was to save the right eye, but the right eye failed steadily during the next year and by 1942 he was almost completely blind. He had to rely utterly upon others to read to him and to take down his letters as he dictated them. He continued his walking but now required an African companion to guide him. The Governor of Rhodesia, Sir Herbert M. Stanley, himself a fine classical scholar, sent Cripps, soon after the loss of his left eye in 1940, a touching poem in Latin to which Cripps's nephew, Hilary Armstrong, on receiving a copy of it from his uncle, sent back his own translation. Two stanzas of it read:

> May you never cease, we pray, unfolding
> Glory of the world in gliding measures,
> While the earth a mirror seems of heaven
>   Lit by your seeing.

> Steadfast in your holy inspiration
> Shield for the poor, scourge for the proud you carry,
> You shall shake oppression's unholy stronghold
>   With your song's battering.

Once again John Snelling included a wide selection of Cripps's poetry in his second anthology *Rhodesian Verse* which B. H. Blackwell's published in 1951 and dedicated the volume to Cripps. G. H. Miller conferred frequently with Cripps in the early years of his blindness about an anthology of verse for the Rhodesian schools that appeared eventually under the title of *Thudding Drums* and included a generous selection of Cripps's own poems.

During the early years of the war, Noel Brettell, a Rhodesian poet of the highest gifts, served as a teacher in the Enkeldoorn school, and in the eighteen months that followed, it is doubtful if Cripps had had such literary company in Africa since his early companionship with Cullen Gouldsbury. Brettel persuaded Cripps to let him ride out on horseback to Maronda Mashona each Thursday afternoon in term-time in order to read poetry to him:

> When I first knew Cripps, he was over seventy and blind ... I had heard of his legend, the astonishing figure that strode the

lonely roads, courteously refusing lifts, and disappearing from surprised stares across the dusty frontiers of the reserves.

Cripps prepared with meticulous care for these readings and Brettell recalls that on the rough table there was always not only tea but a tin of English biscuits or some other delicacy that Cripps never touched himself but had procured especially for his guest!

Cripps was content enough just to listen to my reading. To smoke his pipe, drink his tea, and hear Tennyson was sufficient for our Thursday afternoons.... Apart from Tennyson and some of Gilbert Murry's translations, he left the choice of reading to me.... His memory was phenomenal. To me, equipped with eyes and recent reading, his verbal recall of many passages was often humiliating [For almost four decades Cripps had been repeating poetry aloud by the hour on his endless vigils of walking].... it was grand to think of his shuttered mind so richly furnished.... We read everything—de la Mare one week, Shakespeare another, T. S. Eliot the next ... he was glad for a Housman afternoon.... He was especially pleased when I read some of Vaughan ... Herbert and ... Traherne. In my own reading of his [Cripps's] verse I had felt the affinity.... More vehement than Herbert, not so ecstatic as Vaughan but with a harsher task than either. Cripps's grim features were not often moved as they were then. 'I had never hoped to hear that again', he said.

At the time, Noel Brettell confesses his impatience at Cripps's relentless pressing of the African cause in Rhodesia:

I myself thought we were drifting, but vaguely in the right direction.... That the last twenty years [1945-65] have proved his exaggeration more right than our complacency helps to place him in perspective (From 'Reading to Cripps', in *The Link* (May 1953), and a personal memorandum by Noel Brettell).

Noel Brettell was not the only one who brought some lifting of the curtain of darkness that had settled over Cripps in the final decade of his life. In 1929 while Cripps was still in England, Olive Seth-Smith, a gifted Englishwoman of mature years who had been headmistress of a girls' school in New Zealand, had been invited by the Society of the Divine Compassion at Wreningham to come to assist them in the African women's work. When a reorganization that eliminated her post occurred two years later, she continued in Enkeldoorn with work of her own for African girls. She knew and admired Cripps and ten years later when he became blind she had a small room with its own entrance built on to her house in Enkeldoorn which made it possible for Cripps and an African companion to spend the nights there when they walked in from Maronda Mashanu. She arranged her own affairs so that she could give him the time that was needed to read to him his voluminous post and his papers and books and to type out hundreds of his letters and poems. Cripps called her house, which was such an oasis for him, a Rest Haven, and this became its name. Her gift to him, her rousing of hope that even in his blindness he could go on with his work and his writing of poetry; her sharing, too, his passion for the African people and their unfolding; and in it all, her renunciation of one level of love for another—all of this is here in a whole sheaf of winter verses dedicated to F.O.S.S. that are preserved in the National Archives (N.A.) in Salisbury.

> In the rich autumn of your days
> Befriending in my Winter's woe
>
> I did not tell you of my need
> But in my need you sped to me.

This deep and moving personal devotion that kindled in Cripps all the normal passions and that led him once to confide to a friend that 'This has come too late', might well have run out into the dry sands of pathos, sadness, and lament, like an African river that disappears in the desert. But there are bursts in his poems that see in the renunciation of the normal course of this love not a niggardly and complaining deprivation but a spendthrift gift, joyfully given and abundantly rewarded.

When Olive Seth-Smith was stricken with cancer in 1950, apart from some volunteer periods of assistance from Mrs E. Robb, almost the whole burden of this work as secretary fell upon Leonard Mamvura, and with negligible compensation he quietly and uncomplainingly served Cripps to the very end. In 1945 Cripps had moved heaven and earth to get Leonard Mamvura, an African who had grown up on his farm but who had been away for some further education, to return to Maronda Mashanu in order to fill the teaching vacancy in his principal school. Cripps could hardly have foreseen what this loyal and devoted African teacher would do for him personally in the few remaining years of his life. For Leonard Mamvura was soon not only teaching in the school but also caring for Cripps, bicycling in to Enkeldoorn in the early days of the week which Cripps and his African companion usually spent at Rest Haven, in order to assist the overburdened Olive Seth-Smith in the reading and writing duties that showed no signs of abating. After dark, he cycled the five plus miles back to his small neglected farm to join his family and to prepare his lessons for the next day. One would need to return to the epic faithfulness of Livingstone's African companions who carried his embalmed body encased in bark from Chitambo's village to the coast of the Indian Ocean in order to find a match for the magnificent and competent devotion of Leonard Mamvura to Arthur Cripps in these last seven years of his life.

With this faithful help Cripps in the closing years of his life was able to continue his resistance to the linking of the former territories of Nyasaland and Northern Rhodesia, where in practice there was no colour bar, to Southern Rhodesia. In 1942 he published a widely read pamphlet *Is Our Colour Bar to Cross the Zambesi?* After the close of World War II, he pressed this issue through the more than willing Arthur Creech-Jones, who was now in the Labour Cabinet, and through the Colonial Bureau of the Fabian Society, and the matter seemed to have been damped down. But in 1949 Huggins and Welensky negotiated a conference that took place at Victoria Falls and laid out a plan for the Federation. It is reported that there was not a single African included in the original planning session. By 1953, a year after Cripps's death, the Federation came into being. Cripps's original insight received some vindication a decade later in 1963 when African opposition succeeded in dissolving it and, as Zambia and Malawi, these two territories became independent African nations.

Cripps's close co-operation with Rita Hinden in these latter years with clippings from Rhodesian papers and the Rhodesian Hansard; copies of bills that were being introduced; and documentation of specific injustices to Africans is all on record in the files of the

Colonial Bureau of the Fabian Society. His careful planning helped her to cause Sir Geoffrey Huggins, when in London in 1947, to be visited and warned by a strong British parliamentary delegation of the consequences of his threats to tamper with the African electoral franchise provisions of the Rhodesian constitution, in which Huggins saw a potential threat to white rule. Archbishop Paget wrote to Cripps that after this visitation he believed Huggins might now drop this threat that he had brandished for years.

While Cripps's own health was failing, his financial problems with his farms went from bad to worse. These farms were host to a sizeable group of African families. There were mortgage payments on the farms and threats of foreclosures; overdue fencing loans to the government; notices that dipping regulations, stock control, and a costly programme of contour ploughing were not being complied with. Douglas Aylen, a government official who greatly admired Cripps, tried to help him and sought to persuade some of the African tenants to move with their animals to more favoured situations in the reserves. But Cripps's African friends were reluctant to leave and swift to return. In more than one crisis the African community itself rallied to Cripps's aid and by their collections of sizeable amounts of money helped him to meet the emergency. But relief from his troubles was never more than temporary.

Cripps managed by great personal sacrifices to support the schools on his farms without the aid of government subsidies until 1945. But beyond that point he could no longer make this witness and so turned the management and the finances of the schools over to a small committee of people whom he trusted to receive the public aid and to govern the schools.

Cripps himself was completely impoverished by his ceaseless assistance to the Africans with whom he was surrounded. It is told that on one occasion towards the end of his life, he was led into an Indian shop in Enkeldoorn in order to make a purchase that ran to something like £4, only to discover that he did not have the money on him. He said that he would go to the bank and draw it from his account. The shopkeeper, Mr Desai, who knew that Cripps's bank account was nil and who did not want to have his much-loved friend embarrassed, slipped over to the bank before Cripps could get there and deposited five pounds to Cripps's account so that all would be in order. Only by such subterfuges of love was it possible in these closing years to help Cripps.

There were periodic efforts by now one and now another Anglican woman from Enkeldoorn to wash his blankets and improve his mattress pad or to rescue him in some way from the white ants that ate his paper and the rodents that finished off any left-overs from his meals in the small rondavel at Maronda Mashanu. But nothing could separate him from this place where he could grope his way into the church and celebrate Holy Communion. Nor was there any prying him away from the African families who looked after his minimal needs.

Earlier in 1952, he spent two sizeable periods in the Enkeldoorn hospital and it was there on 1 August of that year that he died. His funeral was a window through which it was possible to catch some glimpse of how much his life had meant to his community.

In his original will and testament Cripps had directed: 'I desire to be buried without a coffin on the hill of Makirri Mawe situated on the farm Muckleneuk in the district of Charter with the rites of the Church of England.' Meanwhile at the foot of that hill, Cripps's beloved Maronda Mashanu church had been built and his friends could not think of any place so suitable as the very centre of its nave as the spot to bury his body. The African has a very deep feeling for the hallowing power of the bones of his ancestors on the very soil into which they are placed. And when a foreign friend of Africa would show that he really cares, the question may be bluntly put, 'Will you leave your bones with us?'

A simple wooden coffin was hammered out in the workshop of the Daramombe Mission and two days later on Sunday, 3 August, Cripps's burial took place. The Anglican periodical, *The Link*, in its September 1962 number dedicated to *Arthur Shearly Cripps— Priest and Poet* contains an eye-witness account of the funeral:

The body lay in the little church of St Cyril [Enkeldoorn], where he used to minister in times past, from eleven on Sunday morning till half-past two when the first part of the service began ... The Congregation of Europeans, Indians, Coloureds and Africans was much too big for the church to hold.... There was no hearse; the coffin was carried in a van lent and driven by Mudiwa Bill, the Enkeldoorn bus proprietor.... From St Cyril's the procession of cars made its way to Maronda Mashanu.

A quarter of a mile from there the cars stopped and the coffin was taken up by the six bearers.

As the pallbearers came to Cripps's 'Jordan', the little stream in which he had baptized hundreds of his African friends,

A vast crowd of Africans was waiting in silence. Suddenly three shots rang out, the women began to wail, and a group of men broke into a war dance and a famous song used only to honour a great chief. [Richard Nash who had played the organ at the St Cyril part of the service says of this moment of song, 'It inspired me to the core, and strangely very closely resembled one of the liveliest themes in the last movement of Beethoven's 9th Symphony'.] Old men, who had long known Father Cripps almost all their lives, took the coffin from the pall bearers and bore it to the Church of the Five Wounds [Maronda Mashanu] while the great company sang hymns, including one in Shona by Father Cripps himself.

A grave had been prepared in the chancel of the church, and there in a service presided over by African priests and conducted in Shona, Arthur Cripps was laid to rest. The next day Cripps's much loved follower whom he had himself drawn into the priesthood, Cyprian Tambo, said a Requiem Mass for his friend and patron, and Leonard Mamvura noted that ninety-seven Africans took Communion. An Anglican colleague chose the poem *Stigmata Amoris* from *Africa: Verses* to sum up Cripps's own departure:

> Now dust to dust! No dust-cloud whirls about
> That white cloud over hills you went so far.
> Now all is grey: set is the last red star:
> Ashes to ashes! Your last fire is out.
>
> Now go, a veldsore in each lifted hand,
> Go with two blistered feet your altar's way,
> With pity's wound at heart, go, praise and pray! ·
> Go, wound to Wounds! Why you are glad today—
> He, whose Five Wounds you wear, will understand.

(p.54)

'Why you are glad today' is the note on which to sum up Cripps's life. It was not the sacrifices, the veld-sores, the loneliness, the failures, the stretches of indecision, the defeats in the struggle to touch the white conscience in Rhodesia and Britain, the decade of blindness, that mattered. David Livingstone who had lost both his beloved wife and a child with fever, who had been mauled by a lion, known almost every taxing hardship which the African bush could inflict, and who himself reports twenty-seven bouts of malarial fever in two and a half years, once insisted that in all his life he had never made a sacrifice. He, with Cripps, had simply done what he most deeply wanted to do! And in the final parting, what else matters?

Both of these irregulars, on the whole so well understood by Africans and yet so little understood by their own white colleagues in the field, were content to follow Unamuno's bidding to 'Sow yourself, sow the living part of yourself in the furrows of life', and to leave the harvest in Another's hands. Both men believed that the tally was not yet in, and that 'He whose Five Wounds you wear, will understand'.

Index